C000066866

Table of Contents

"Becoming wealthy may be unachievable,
but living debt free is absolutely attainable"
- Dr. Howard B. Slaughter, Jr.

ADDICTED TO DEBT

Get Out and Stay Out!

Dr. Howard B. Slaughter, Jr.

Addicted to Debt
by Howard B. Slaughter, Jr.
Copyright © 2019 Christian Management Enterprises, LLC

ISBN # 978-1-63360-111-6

Scriptures are taken from the KING JAMES VERSION (KJV), public domain.

For Worldwide Distribution Printed in the U.S.A.

Urban Press
P.O. Box 8881
Pittsburgh, PA 15221-0881 USA
412.646.2780
www.urbanpress.us

FOREWORD

I've known Howard Slaughter for more than 30 years and I'm delighted that he is writing this book, but not just any book. It's a book that is needed, as he will tell you again and again, our country is in a financial dilemma because we as a nation are addicted to debt.

My father started a business that now has national acclaim. In fact, we are the fourth largest real estate company in America. We have built our business by providing quality homes for people of varying incomes, ethnicities, and locations, and we know the importance of limited-to-no debt, which makes it easier to qualify for a mortgage. That's why I am endorsing this book and its advice, because we understand the importance of good money and debt management for people to achieve their dream of home-ownership, something most Americans still strive to attain.

We have witnessed the pain and misery a foreclosure can bring, and some occurred as a result of the downturn in the 2008 economy along with other unforeseen economic and personal circumstances. The sad reality is some foreclosures were due to people who did not effectively manage what they had. This is a gloomy commentary and result of their inability to manage their own financial resources.

A home is often the largest asset a family or individual will have, which is why we are in the business of providing quality homes for families across America, which often begins with financial advice and budgeting. We work with people to help them qualify for their homes. That's where Howard comes in, he has written this book, which is replete with wisdom that I know everyone can benefit from. Howard has the experience, passion, and knowledge that will enable you as you read this book to make smart money moves and eventually become and live debt free.

Howard Slaughter is not only a trusted colleague, but he is also a friend. He's been a consultant for our firm and now serves on the board of directors for the Howard Hanna Free Care Fund Foundation, which gives millions of dollars annually to hospitals around the country for child treatments and care. We have chosen our advisers and directors carefully, and Howard has been on our board since its inception. I was also chairman of Howard's advisory board of Fannie Mae's Southwestern Pennsylvania Business Center where he served for seven years as the regional director.

This book is well-written and provides many personal examples of practical money management skills, but the principles will only work if you apply them. Knowing about financial management is not enough; it must be applied and often under difficult circumstances and pressures that may cause you to ignore what you know is best, but you shouldn't. I urge you to read this book with the intent to do what Howard recommends. If you do, it will bring peace, and a sense of stability and happiness to you and your loved ones for generations to come.

Thank you, Howard, for taking what you've learned over the years and sharing that information with the public at large. I hope people will realize what a treasure you are to so many individuals around the country. I also hope you will continue on this phenomenal trajectory. When you asked me to write this foreword, I was extremely pleased to do so. I look forward to continuing our friendship and working relationship for many years to come.

Howard W. "Hoddy" Hanna, III
Chairman, Howard Hanna Real Estate Services

INTRODUCTION

Only one of every four Americans indicate they are debt-free accordingly to CNBC.com. Since the average American household has $137,063 in debt (according to the Federal Reserve), and the U.S. Census Bureau reported the 2016 median household income was $59,039, it is easy to conclude that many Americans are living beyond their means. When we look at bank accounts and retirement savings, the median American household has $11,700 in savings, according to MagnifyMoney.com, with almost 30% of households having less than $1,000 in savings. More than two of every three American adults (68%) who are in debt doubt they will ever live debt-free, according to CreditCards.com in a survey of 1,114 American adults. Almost 31 million Americans with credit card debt think they will die with debt.

With evidence like this, I thought it time to sound the alarm in a pragmatic way and discuss American consumers' addiction to debt. If more than 50% of Americans were addicted to drugs or alcohol, it would be considered a national emergency, a crisis, or even an epidemic. The current reality is that a majority of Americans are living with some kind of debt, which they believe is normal, so they have relegated themselves to a lifelong relationship with debt.

I am not implying that everyone who has incurred debt is addicted. What I am saying, however, is the data indicates that more people are addicted to debt and they don't realize it. Let's make it even more personal. If you take on debt to maintain the lifestyle you are living and don't have any way to reduce it or a budget you stick to, you could be addicted. The Joneses are no longer the family some aspire to be like; today it's a new family called the technologists. This family has all the latest gadgets and spares no cost to get them. They know the tech lingo and they keep up with all the happenings on social media, but fail to realize purchasing all the latest tech tools is costly and this insatiable desire to keep up at any cost can be addictive, and often is.

Being addicted to debt is frightening because no household can exist without handling money. What's more, debt is legal. With so many ads for items to purchase, vacations, new living room furniture, or to fund your child's education, it seems so right, but it can be so wrong if you don't know how to handle debt. Debt addiction is at its worst when people are making minimum payments on what they owe or when they are using the balance from one card to pay off another. The worst part of any addiction is the denial that goes along with it.

If you need four or more credit cards to support your lifestyle, is it the credit card company's fault who gave you four or more cards, or is it your fault for falling victim to your own debt addiction? If you derive comfort from simply knowing you have those cards in your wallet or purse, this is an indication you may be getting addicted and on the verge of having a financial setback or crisis because you do not have adequate savings to cover the payments associated with the use of the cards.

Furthermore, if you need to use your credit card to purchase something that costs $15, it's probably something you should not buy if you are not able to pay cash. A credit card is easy to use, and the problem is that you don't feel the $300 purchase until later. If you use cash, you feel the impact of your purchase immediately. With the card, you can have what you want *right now* and not have to wait. That's where the addiction begins and for some consumers, it just doesn't stop. When it is for something that costs much more than a $15 purchase, it doesn't take long before you are overwhelmed, over budget, and over your head in debt.

Debt is Marketed Like Other Products

Credit card companies are shrewd marketers, using catchy jingles in their commercials or tricky introductory rates to lure consumers into accepting and then using their credit cards. They want to soften the effects of debt and entice you into being comfortable with their products. For example, some give you cash back on your purchases and act like it is a bonus of some kind, which it is not. If you get 1.5% back on any purchases you make with a certain card and make a $1,000 purchase, the cash back amounts to $15. If you are going to pay off that $1,000 purchase right away, that is a benefit to you. If you don't, however, then you may end up paying hundreds of dollars in interest and the $15 cash back won't amount to much. Other companies give you points to use toward purchases or travel for every dollar you spend. They want you using their card and if you are not able to pay the balance off every month, they have you right where they want you.

Still other companies treat the card like a commodity by putting a university name, school colors, or the logo of your favorite sports team on the front, like it is something you would show off or that has some type of value to it, even though it's a thin piece of plastic (or in some cases even metal) with an embedded memory chip. They don't want you seeing the card as something dangerous, but rather as something like a friend or tool to help you or give you something back in return for your loyalty. They may give your alma mater a 1% contribution of all your purchases, designed to make you feel like you are doing some good when you spend more than you make.

Consumers often don't recognize the danger until it's too late. They don't see what they are doing is harmful to themselves, but they can't help themselves. If a credit card comes in the mail box or via email approval, they're going to take it. If a gas card comes, they are going to use it. There are many people today who swipe the card and deal with the consequences later. In many cases, these credit card companies are flexible enough that if someone doesn't pay on time, they don't immediately get cut off from the use of the card. If someone is over the limit, the lender charges an over-the-limit fee, which can be a net profit for the credit card company. In many cases, they don't discourage the practice of going over the limit; they make money from it.

When someone is addicted to debt, all the other financial practices go out the window. You can balance your checkbook, but you can't really save or invest when you are addicted. You are under pressure and stress and that can cause you to make more bad financial decisions. That's why this addiction is so serious and has dramatic repercussions, just like an addiction to food, drugs, alcohol, pornography, or opioids would.

The problem isn't just with credit cards, but also with consumer loans, mortgages, school loans, and any other practices that involve borrowing money and paying interest. If you take out a second mortgage on your home and then use the money to go on a vacation, is that economically viable? This is using money for something with no long-term benefit. Once the vacation is over, all you have is the memories, and the bill to prove it. There is no value that can appreciate and increase over time with this type of transaction.

Because we are a nation of people in debt, the nation itself is in debt too. As I write this book, the U.S. is $22,000,000,000,000 in debt and by the time you read this book, we will be in even more debt. As a country, we are never going to repay the trillions of dollars we are borrowing and spending. We will just pass it off to the next generation for them to worry about. Some consumers have the same attitude toward personal debt. Haven't you heard people say, "I'm always going to have a car payment," and they begin to get comfortable with that idea, no longer alarmed at the thought?

Dr. Howard B. Slaughter, Jr.

The Problems with Debt Are Many

If this book does nothing else, I want you to think when you finish, "I don't have to live this way. I don't have to have a new car every three or four years. I don't need the latest fad, gadget, or smartphone upgrade." I want you to think about having a positive and not a negative net worth. You may ask how it's possible to have a negative net worth. I will explain later, but I assure you it is possible.

Debt puts people in the worst position they could ever be in, and in many cases, people never come out of it. As a result, people are compelled to do different things to get money. People start making bad decisions. They gamble on get-rich-quick schemes, including gambling itself. They start a second business, but it's not that easy when you have another job that's already stressful. Another cause of the debt addiction is immense financial illiteracy. The average American does not have basic knowledge about savings, investments, budgeting, and the cost of debt, but many believe they do, which is another problem.

Think about this. If the average American saved $2,085 a month from the time he or she was twenty years old, that person would be a millionaire by the time they are 60. Americans don't focus on savings; only two percent of Americans save regularly. When people get to retirement age, in many cases, they don't have enough money to live on so they can't retire or if they do, they can't retire comfortably. They are working until they're 75 and it's not all just because they want to do it, but because they don't have enough income to support themselves.

Today, most American high schools do not have any requirements to teach anything related to consumer finances. Students take algebra, calculus, and maybe even trigonometry, but most schools do not teach anything about how to manage money, something the students will be doing a few years out of school. Right after school, someone is going to offer them a credit card, telling them to sign and use it.

Those young adults sometimes spend $1,200 on clothes, make the minimum payments, and end up paying $1,600 for jeans and sneakers. Before they know it, the clothes are out of style and the cycle begins all over again. Then they get their next card and if they are not disciplined, they will soon be in trouble and the addiction has been actualized. I have heard people advise folks to cut up their cards. That sounds good, but the credit card companies are relentless and will send you another credit card. Cutting the card up won't solve the problem because it's deeper than what a pair of scissors can do.

It's a difficult conversation to tell people they are addicted. They don't want to hear it and don't believe it. I want you to recognize for yourself if and when you are in that situation, because only at that point can you figure out how to get out and stay out. I want you to understand the dilemma you are in before it worsens. Before you can do something about it, you must first recognize and acknowledge it.

Debt Free, Then Set Free

When you are free of debt, when you get out and stay out, you aren't stressed, that has psychological and emotive benefits. The benefits are health and wellness to your body and psyche. You don't have to be a millionaire to enjoy these benefits. Getting out of debt allows you to move freely and to make better choices and decisions. You will have more dollars in your savings account if you don't have any debt. You can open a checking account with enough money so you don't have to pay any fees.

More importantly, when you don't have debt, you are able to make smarter choices than you would otherwise be able to make if you had debt. For me, the biggest benefit of being debt free is no stress. You work differently and with less pressure when you owe no one anything. The Bible actually teaches that we are to "owe no man anything" (see Romans 13:8). You begin to save even more because you know the benefits of being free, so you begin walking away from debt choices. Once you are out of debt, you won't want to pay a car note again or have a second mortgage; you will like the freedom that no monthly payments gives you. You can't realize or appreciate the benefits until you are there.

You must believe it is possible and have the discipline to set the goal to be debt free and then move forward to attain it. Average Americans do not believe they can become set free; this is evidenced by the reality that most Americans remain in debt. You must start with believing. If you can't see yourself debt free, expect to be debt-laden for the rest of your life. No one can take this step for you; it is a God-inspired moment, which only comes by prayer and faith, then appropriate action.

Debt Does Not Discriminate

Why it is that debt seems uncontrollable regardless of a person's income level? It seems plausible that someone with lower income may have more challenges to maintain a budget while dealing with the necessities of life. We tend to excuse a person in that situation, even though we shouldn't. Debt does not discriminate; it attacks all income levels and the implications are the same for everyone, no matter what your income level is. How often have we heard about a person who made millions but is broke? The myth that it has something to do with someone's income is just that, a myth. Becoming debt free is a journey that anyone can achieve, even you, so there is no excuse for you to still be in debt.

Debt, no matter anyone's socioeconomic status, remains a daunting and elusive goal to achieve, and many don't believe they can achieve it. Do not assume high-income earners are exempt from the debt problem. Many of these individuals do not live the set-free, debt-free life. Higher-income earners can mask their high debt load because these individuals have more disposable income to pay toward their debt, but they can also experience problems in paying their debt off just like anyone else and sometimes do.

A high income is not synonymous with being debt free. In some cases, high-income earners assume even more risk because of their income, and that can be a big mistake. They can get lulled to sleep at times by creditors because they often receive higher credit limits, and can purchase larger vehicles or homes, based on their income

God has blessed my wife and I to be set free, so I know anyone can become set free by becoming debt free. Set free can mean different things to people, but for me it meant keeping a home for my family under any adverse circumstances that may arise. It meant not having to worry about losing my home in the event of a job change or loss of income. The home is the largest asset most people own, so it's worth protecting. By owning, you are protecting, but by amassing more debt, you're jeopardizing your financial future. You may not ever regain your financial footing and recover from a loss of such a sizable asset.

How challenging was my situation? What qualifies me to tell you that you can get free? On the following page is my actual budget from 1991, which includes my debt picture and many monthly payments. We were ultimately set free because we became debt free, but it wasn't easy.

You Need a Plan

Being debt free is a personal choice and journey, one that takes thoughtful planning, a committed and dedicated family consensus, and most importantly, prayer. Without a strategy, the likelihood is that you'll remain burdened with debt. I will refer to a passage of Scriptures throughout this book. James 2:26 says, "But wilt thou know, O vain man, that faith without works is dead?". While you have faith that God can relieve your debt, you must do the work to accompany your faith. The plan and commitment to the goal of becoming debt free requires a debt-free plan that you must work. It won't happen by osmosis. Take control of your future by investing

	The Family Budget			November 1, 1991
Lender	Balance	Payment	Due Date	Remaining payments
Mortgage	$57,803	$716.00	1	324
GMAC	$ 3,675	$334.00	30	11
Home Equity 2nd Mortgage	$24,963	$289.44	16	61
Bank Signature loan	$14,300	$138.84	16	102
Household Finance Corp.	$ 7,855	$157.00	12	50
Bank Overdraft Protection	$ 2,000	$ 55.00	25	36
Bank One	$ 4,000	$100.00	4	40
N.A.C.O.	$ 1,900	$ 31.00	1	61
Bank of Hoven	$ 400	$ 22.00	30	18
Finance Corporation	$ 2,500	$139.00	9	18
Finance Corporation	$ 1,700	$106.00	14	16
Montgomery Ward	$ 533	$ 21.00	14	25
Radio Shack	$ 1,489	$ 48.00	21	31
Credit Card	$ 1,500	$ 62.00	20	24
Kaufman's	$ 199	$ 25.00	10	8
Beneficial	$ 3,000	$ 87.00	3	34
Blazer Financial	$ 2,800	$110.00	10	27
Citibank Platinum Visa	$ 2,950	$ 99.00	1	29
Car Insurance	$ 1,260	$105.00	5	12
Gas Card	$ 317	$ 35.00	4	9

1st   Mortgage w/ 30 year amortization totals $716.00 x 360 = $257,760.00

2nd   Mortgage w/15 year amortization totals $ 289.44 x 180 = $ 52,099.20

Total debt payments if mortgages were not paid off early   **$309,859.20**

in yourself today, but not through just more investments, but by eliminating debt. The liberation from undue pressure is what sets you free.

The reason most people remain in debt is because they are undisciplined when it comes to their finances. To become set free requires time, a plan, and a commitment to change the way you operate. Yes, they can complete a degree, they can still go to work, but what they can't do is stop thinking and stressing about what to do with the money they owe, which impacts everything. Over time, it erodes their very life and this is what every person needs to be set free from.

This includes all walks of life, from the pulpit to the pew, from the chief executive officer to the janitor, from the professional athletes to high school students. Debt does not discriminate; it affects most people. It likes to linger as long as it can, is no respecter of persons, and is slippery. According to My Daily Informer, 43 percent of American families spend more money than they earn on an annual basis and the average household carries about $8,000 in credit card debt.

What You Can Expect When Reading This Book

This book is in two sections. I will start with one chapter that explains my journey and background that prepared me to write about debt and finances. I will tell you more about my personal journey into and out of debt, and the depth of the debt problem in this nation. I will also draw on my experience as a banker, adjunct professor, entrepreneur and Christian over the past 38 years. I learned a lot over the years, some of what I learned had a profound impact on me, although I still had a lot to learn about handling my finances effectively. A principle worth remembering is this: God owns everything, we own nothing. He has given us authority to manage what He has given us and we ought to do so with grace, gratitude, and a giving heart.

The first section is the longest section and is going to include material on financial literacy. You may think, "I have a master's degree, I don't need to read this section," but I beg to differ. Even if you handle millions of dollars for your company or command a handsome salary, you need a brush-up course on the basics of consumer finances. The second section will be my remedy for the addiction along with the prevention for the same. It will discuss values and takes a closer look at what the Bible says about finances and money, including generosity.

I was an adjunct professor at the University of Pittsburgh, Point Park University, and Community College of Allegheny County where I taught business management, diversity in public service, and other courses to college students. It became evident early on that students matriculated into college without any formal training in money management.

Most high schools in America do not require any consumer finances courses as a prerequisite for graduating from high school. That means the educated are uneducated or undereducated when it comes to handling their finances, which sounds oxymoronic. In fact, many go through high school and college and never take a class on finances, so how educated are these individuals? If you don't understand the basic principles of finances, are you truly ready for society? Is society better off by graduating students, many of whom don't know how to read a balance sheet or income statement, and who don't know how to prepare a net worth statement, or balance their own checkbooks?

In 2006, I had the opportunity to address this problem and I will share some of the results and my experience with you in section two. I earned a Doctor of Science Degree in Information Systems and Communications from Robert Morris University and my doctoral dissertation was titled *"Financial Illiteracy; an American Epidemic: A Qualitative Study on the Effectiveness of Web-Based Financial Literacy Technology Training on African-American High School Students in Pittsburgh."*

In my doctoral dissertation, I did an analysis of how well high school students understood credit when I administered a pre- and post-test on financial literacy. I engaged students from Pittsburgh public high schools and local churches in urban Pittsburgh. My hypothesis was that if we take individuals who have no concept of credit and finances and give them a week's worth of training, there would be an increase in learning. My hypothesis was proven accurate, one week of training did indeed make a significant difference in their understanding of finances.

I had nearly forty co-researchers (the students) as we called them. I raised funds from a foundation and hired bankers, African-Americans with PhDs for a week-long summer financial literacy boot camp at Robert Morris University. I hired a facilitator and an executive director, and we did this each year for two consecutive years. For those two years, we brought the students to the university for classes by day and sponsored fun things in the evening since the students stayed on campus. We measured their progress by giving them a pre-session and then a post-session quiz.

Here's an important thing that emerged from the research. When we started to do this, I had the students go home and talk with their parents about what they learned. I then started to get calls from parents asking what we were teaching their kids. It wasn't that they were concerned. In many cases, parents didn't understand what we were teaching the students. We found out that parents often wanted to help their kids, but they were giving them incorrect information in some instances.

Therefore, I decided to bring the parents in for their own program. We taught them what we were teaching their children. It was a way for them to get help to understand what was being taught. In many cases, the parents never had any kind of financial training themselves. I call it financial literacy education and I will share some of that training with you in section two of this book. If you are a parent, you have a big part to play in your child's financial future.

Some of these students have gone on to have great careers. One participant went to Stanford, another started a business, and one currently works for a bank. When I gave away what I knew, it enabled others to benefit. I was blessed because I ended up with the research I needed for my dissertation, and it was fun and exciting. The real benefit for me was being able to teach more than 100 students, and empower the team we hired. Because I was giving, God gave me. I blessed other people, and those blessings came back to me. I will discuss the mentality of giving in the second section.

Let's get started by addressing the not-so-happy problems many of our citizens are facing as they struggle with an excessive amount of debt. Before they can be set free, they must be debt free, and before they can be debt free, they must face how high that mountain of debt is. There is no way around it, so let's climb it together and trust that by the end of this book, you will be set free, never to turn or return to a life of debt.

All financial calculations in this book are for illustrative purposes only and not absolute.

Dr. Howard B. Slaughter, Jr., MBA, MPM
Pittsburgh, PA
April 2019

Chapter 1
My Journey

Growing up in a tough urban environment wasn't easy. I had no post-high school education until I was 31. Living in deplorable conditions didn't help either. A loving mother who worked hard and scrubbed floors for a wealthy family in Squirrel Hill and taught me the principles of God and helped me learn how to achieve. Let me share a little of my journey with you.

I grew up in the Homewood and Garfield sections of Pittsburgh. My mother told me a few years ago that when I was five years old, she was walking me down the street one day when I said, "Mommy, if I had money, I'd fix up all these houses for people." How prophetic that was because I ultimately became the regional director for Fannie Mae with a two-billion-dollar housing plan goal for all of Southwestern Pennsylvania. I led that effort for seven years and helped 24,000 individuals and families become homeowners.

Today, I am president and chief executive officer of Habitat for Humanity of Greater Pittsburgh, whose mission is to build and repair homes for low- and limited-income families. God has blessed me to be involved in my purpose, and He has opened many doors for me. All of it is by God's grace, but I prepared myself to the best of my ability, all the while following certain principles that took me from a high school graduate to the chief executive officer of three different organizations along with the achievement of five earned degrees. I want to share what I have learned with you in this book.

We were poor in Homewood, and I was raised for 15 years in a single-parent household. When I graduated from high school, my mother said, "You can't stay here and not work." I was not ready for Post High School education, even though I did well in school. What's more, there was no money to send me to college. Since I had no scholarship offers, I went into the United States Navy to get experience and take advantage of the GI Bill to go to school later. Two weeks after my high school graduation, I found myself at Great Lakes, Illinois, adjusting to life with 80 other men, sleeping on a hard bunk, with no comforts of home like television. It is known as boot camp.

The Lord brought me through all that to where I am today. Our success is not predicated on who our parents are or are not. It's not determined by what side of the tracks we lived on (or didn't). Our success is and will be based on following the principles God has established. If we do that, we will find our way out of where we are to where we want to be. There is no magic formula or shortcut. It's faith and works, and it has nothing to do with the economy, race, or political affiliation. The Bible says, "Faith without works is dead" (James 2:26). There is no interpretation needed for this verse!

Given the volatility of the stock market and the fact that in twenty years there will probably be no Social Security program, there are things you must do now to ensure you are financially stable in the future. The average person gains much of his or her wealth from the equity in their home. That's all well and good if someone owns a home, but as of 2016, African-American homeownership was 41.7%, near a 50-year low according to the U.S. Census Bureau. African Americans are near the bottom of the rung as far as their wealth and net worth are concerned.

I want you to understand and believe that you can get there (financial stability and debt-free living) from wherever you are now. If you believe in and follow God's principles, you will find the way out of where you are and onto where you want to be. When my wife and I became debt-free, I cannot describe how liberating it was. I want you to experience that same feeling too.

My Job at Equibank

In high school, I needed to take one more class and the only option was a home economics or typing class. My mother encouraged me to take the typing course. No guy took typing in the mid-1970s in high school, but reluctantly, I took the course. That class provided an important path for my life, starting when I enlisted. I became a Navy yeoman, an administrative position, because I could type 60 words per minute with no mistakes.

It is interesting that after getting assigned to the U.S.S Hunley (AS-31) and being stationed in Charleston, South Carolina for two years, I received orders to go to Guam. At the time, I didn't know where Guam was, nor did I want to go. Then I received a second set of orders out of the blue that surprised me and countermanded the Guam orders. I was given a new assignment in Washington, D.C. after I was investigated by the FBI. I was being assigned to the Department of Defense, specifically in the Defense Intelligence Agency, to a group that prepared intelligence notes for the Secretary of Defense, Harold Brown, during the Carter Administration. This required a top secret clearance, which I received after the FBI investigation. I had excellent administrative skills, notwithstanding I was a yeoman.

We worked seven days on night shift, and three of those days were twelve-hour shifts, but we were off the following seven days. That meant I only worked two weeks a month and had 30 days of paid vacation. I only worked five months a year and thought I had arrived. After a long-term illness of my stepfather, I left Washington to come home to assist my mother. I am her only child and felt obligated to do so, but it was all in God's plan.

When I arrived back in Pittsburgh, I applied for a job at a local bank named Equibank, and they asked me what I could do. I couldn't do much but I told them I could type. I ended up being the first male customer service representative the bank had ever hired, and also became a teller. Ultimately, as I was trying to move up the corporate ladder, I spent some time in the collections department as a bill collector. I had to do some of the things other people didn't want to do, and one of them was to be a bill collector.

Every day, my job was to call the people who were behind on their credit card or loan payments. We used to call it dialing for dollars. I did that all day every day, and I got to be good at it, not realizing I would benefit from understanding the problems people face with an abundance of debt. We used all kind of tactics to get people to pay. I learned that it's not pretty when someone owes money, and my job was not to extend mercy or grace. It was to collect the bank's money.

We would call people's neighbors if they didn't return our calls. We would call Mrs. Whomever, the lady who lived next door to the person who owed the bank, and say, "I can't reach John, your neighbor. Can you give him a message for me please? This is Howard at this number." We didn't say we were with the bank. The neighbors were happy to do that, thinking they were helping us find somebody and helping their neighbor too. The consumer knew who Howard was, and they knew the number. They were compelled to call because they didn't want us to keep calling their neighbors. My point is that I learned early on how important it is to manage your debt. I was so good at collections that they moved me into an area where we did repossessions for those who ultimately refused or were unable to pay.

We had a dentist who wouldn't pay us the money he had borrowed to buy a dental chair. We showed up at his office and were going to repossess the chair if he didn't pay. Somebody had a yacht and we repossessed it, going to the dock to secure it. It showed me that someone who was a dentist or another professional had to learn how to manage their debt, even though they were high-income earners. I learned early in life about the consequences of not paying your bills on time.

It wasn't always fun to call people and demand payment, because some had legitimate circumstances preventing them from paying. The bank's perspective, however, was that the person borrowed the money and had promised to pay it back, and the time had come and passed to pay it back. I was the person in the middle, talking to people and hearing their stories, but the bank wanted payment. The people had promised to pay and the bank was holding them and their collateral liable.

The financial challenges were common to almost every profession, regardless of economic status or position. There were pastors and church leaders who had problems Some presidents of companies, an athlete, and a medical professional who still did not know how to manage their finances. It had nothing to do with position, but everything to do with positioning.

You Can't Tell by Observing

You can't judge where someone is based on what you see. There are a lot of people who live in a beautiful home but have significant debt, or who drive a nice car but are just two blocks away from the repo man. I remember being in someone's home that had a pool in the backyard, but no furniture in the living room. It looked like they were living quite well. You don't know who is close to bankruptcy by outward appearances. Debt doesn't care who you are.

That's why I believe not having debt at all, no matter where you fall on the spectrum of money management, is the best way to live. It means you don't have to worry about phone calls or somebody trying to foreclose on your home. It's difficult to recover once you have lost a home through foreclosure, had a car repossessed, or had some other unfortunate circumstance happen to you. It's not a great feeling, and there aren't a lot of people who can come back from those things, although it is possible. If you understand the concepts I will present in this book, and discipline yourself to follow the principles of debt-free living, you can eliminate your debt and not have to worry about loss or financial setbacks.

Is it better to own a mansion and worry or to own something less than a mansion and not have to worry? That's an individual choice, but in my house, we'd rather own less and owe nothing than own more and owe more. It's an individual preference, but once you get to the point where you are debt-free, it's hard to go back into debt again because you recognize the freedom and the choices you have and the things that you can do are so much more, like helping others, giving to the ministry, and enjoying stress-free living.

Debt brings stress, and stress brings on a whole new set of burdens. Not being able to manage your money can lead to personal problems. Mismanagement of money is one of the leading causes of problems in marriages today.

FICO

People know that having a high Fair Isaac Company (FICO) credit score is preferable. (FICO is the California Company that uses an undisclosed algorithm to calculate a credit score for each citizen, which is then used by lending institutions as a guide to their credit offers). I remember a time, however, when there was no such thing as a credit score. As a bank manager and consumer lender, I would pull credit reports and do an assessment based on what people owed, what they owned, how much debt and income they had, and how timely their payments were. Today, loan officers no longer do their work that way.

By the way, no one can tell you how those FICO scores are comprised. We do know the score is based on debt. People get a higher score when they pay their bills on time. You must have debt to get a score so you have access to more debt. You want a higher score but that means you need to borrow in order to repay. Then if you pay on time, it's likely your score will increase. You don't want to have debt just to get a higher score, but that's the principle involved in credit scoring. On the following pages, I am including two letters from 2009 to show you the mysterious ways that FICO scores are calculated. As you will see, my score went down because I did not use a credit card, which is counterintuitive to the idea of a better score for good money management skills.

www.myfico.com

200 Smith Ranch Road
San Rafael, CA 94903-5551

September 15, 2009

Dr. Howard Slaughter

Dear Dr. Slaughter,

Per your request for a written summary of our recent phone conversation of September 10, 2009, regarding your FICO credit score, the following is an explanation of why your Equifax FICO score dropped from 798 on June 30, 2009 to 788, as of August 28, 2009.

To clarify the role of the Fair Isaac Corporation (FICO®) in the credit scoring process, we developed the FICO® credit scoring formula, a proprietary algorithm that is widely used to calculate consumer credit scores. FICO scores range from 300 to 850, with higher scores indicating lower future credit risk. While Fair Isaac developed the FICO scoring models used by the three national credit bureaus – Equifax, Experian and TransUnion – we do not collect credit or public record information, nor do we determine the content or the accuracy of such information collected by the credit bureaus.

Based on my evaluation of your June 30th and August 28th Equifax credit reports and FICO scores, it appears that the closing of your Citibank credit card account (opened in February 1991) at some point between these two dates negatively impacted your FICO score, as the closure of this account served to reduce the overall amount of revolving credit being made available to you. The amount of credit you have available to use -- along with payment history, amounts owed, length of credit history, and other factors – is just one of many predictive pieces of credit information used by the FICO scoring formula to provide lenders with an estimation of future credit risk.

As I emphasized to you in our conversation, both scores – 798 and 788 -- are indicative of very low risk and can be expected to help you obtain the best credit terms available when applying for credit. I also advised that such minor fluctuations in FICO scores are normal and can be expected when such actions as closing accounts occur.

Please feel free to contact me if you have any additional questions or concerns.

Sincerely,

Consumer Operations Manager

It's not only about getting out of debt; you must learn how to stay out as well. A lot of people achieve that goal, but then go right back into debt, and we will cover principles to prevent that from happening. As you read this book, understand that it is not a how-to book, but a why-not book. This is a lifestyle, based on Christian principles that work.

What the Bible Says

Let's take a quick look at some verses from the Bible that pertain to

Citibank (South Dakota), N.A.
Office of the President
P.O. Box 6000
Sioux Falls, SD 57117-6000

October 5, 2009

Dr. Howard B. Slaughter, Jr.

Citi® Platinum Select® Card
Acct. #5424

Dear Dr. Slaughter:

Thank you for contacting our executive offices regarding your Citi® Platinum Select® Card.

I understand you are concerned with the closure of the above referenced account, as you indicate it affected your FICO score. As part of our Credit review process, an account with no activity for an extended period of time is automatically closed for security reasons. Our records indicate we closed your account in May 2009 due to inactivity. Let me assure you, it was not our intention to inconvenience you in any way. As we are not a credit reporting agency, we are unable to advise customers how an account closure will affect their credit score.

If you would like us to review the account for reopening with a higher line of credit, please notify our office of your request. A self-addressed envelope is enclosed for your convenience. Upon a review of your credit profile, we will notify you of our decision.

I trust this response will lead to a satisfactory resolution of your concerns related to your credit profile.

Sincerely,

Presidential Communications

Enclosure

Federal Regulations Require the Statement Printed on the Reverse Side

the topic at hand: debt and debt-free living:

- Owe no man any thing, but to love one another: for he that loveth another hath fulfilled the law (Romans 13:8).
- The wicked borroweth, and payeth not again: but the righteous sheweth mercy, and giveth (Psalm 37:21).
- "No man can serve two masters: for either he will hate the one, and love the other; or else he will hold to the one, and despise the other. Ye cannot serve God and mammon" (Matthew 6:24).
- Wealth gotten by vanity shall be diminished: but he that gathereth by labour shall increase (Proverbs 13:11).

- "For the Lord thy God blesseth thee, as he promised thee: and thou shalt lend unto many nations, but thou shalt not borrow; and thou shalt reign over many nations, but they shall not reign over thee" (Deuteronomy 15:6).
- Be not thou one of them that strike hands, or of them that are sureties for debts. If thou hast nothing to pay, why should he take away thy bed from under thee? (Proverbs 22:26-27).
- He that loveth silver shall not be satisfied with silver; nor he that loveth abundance with increase: this is also vanity (Ecclesiastes 5:10).
- He that is surety for a stranger shall smart for it: and he that hateth suretiship is sure (Proverbs 11:15)
- "Therefore take no thought, saying, What shall we eat? or, What shall we drink? or, Wherewithal shall we be clothed? (For after all these things do the Gentiles seek:) for your heavenly Father knoweth that ye have need of all these things. But seek ye first the kingdom of God, and his righteousness; and all these things shall be added unto you" (Matthew 6:31-33).
- For the love of money is the root of all evil: which while some coveted after, they have erred from the faith, and pierced themselves through with many sorrows (1 Timothy 6:10).
- A good man leaveth an inheritance to his children's children: and the wealth of the sinner is laid up for the just (Proverbs 13:22).

There are a lot of principles in this list, and I will cover some in detail in this book. The Bible warns against greed, debt, co-signing for someone else's debt, and worrying about finances, which often leads to bad decisions. The Bible's answer for greedy and worry is generosity, found in Luke 6:38, "Give, and it shall be given unto you; good measure, pressed down, and shaken together, and running over, shall men give into your bosom. For with the same measure that ye mete withal, it shall be measured to you again."

Debt in the United States

Here are some statistics that are meant to shock you before we move on (keep in mind these are estimates based on a specific time period and change over time, so you may search and discover different numbers):

- More than 189 million Americans have credit cards.
- The average credit card holder has at least three cards.

- On average, each household with a credit card carries more than $15,000 in credit card debt.
- Total U.S. consumer debt is at $11.4 trillion. That includes mortgages, auto loans, credit cards, and student loans.

Here is what you need to know about student loan debt (source: debt.org):

- Student loan debt has soared from $260 billion in 2004 to $1.4 trillion in 2017.
- Average debt jumped from $18,650 to $38,000 over that same period.
- The number of people over 60 with student loan debt has quadrupled in the last decade from 700,000 to 2.8 million.
- That group's share of the debt has skyrocketed from $8 billion to $67 billion and many are having loan payments deducted from their Social Security checks.
- The average student loan debt for 2016 college graduates who borrowed to get through school was $37,172.

Author's note: Don't ignore the fact that if you owe government student loan debt, you cannot absolve yourself from paying what you owe. Even bankruptcy doesn't negate what you owe the government. Student-loan debt can also be garnished from your pay and even social security.

It doesn't take a math expert to add all this up and realize that Americans are floundering, maybe even drowning, in debt. Are you in this situation? If so, then I want to begin talking to you about what I call financial literacy. We will begin with the concept of making money and then cover the following topics: advertising and values, mortgages, credit cards, predatory lending, and savings. No matter how much you think you know, I would advise you not to skip over any of the chapters, you'll need a good foundation if you are going to overcome or avoid an addiction to debt. Let's get started.

"My grandmother told me,
never be in debt to anyone or anything.
Which is probably why I've never been
financially extravagant. I still go to Costco;
I'm always conscious of living within my means."
- Jill Scott

Section One
Financial Savviness

"I made a commitment to completely cut out drinking
and anything that might hamper me
from getting my mind and body together.
And the floodgates of goodness have opened
upon me both spiritually and financially."
- Denzel Washington

Chapter 2
Advertising and Values

I know what you are thinking: *I thought this section addressed financial savviness? Why are we starting with a discussion about advertising?* I know it seems paradoxical, but advertising plays a key role in an addiction to debt. It is subtle, sophisticated, and well-funded and comes at you through many different lenses that are impossible to escape. The Apostle Paul wrote a well-known warning in Romans 12:1-2 that we need to fully grasp as we begin:

> I beseech you therefore, brethren, by the mercies of God, that ye present your bodies a living sacrifice, holy, acceptable unto God, which is your reasonable service. And be not conformed to this world: but be ye transformed by the renewing of your mind, that ye may prove what is that good, and acceptable, and perfect, will of God.

Look at some phrases in these verses more closely. Paul urged us not to "conform to this world." Culture is often how we make our daily decisions and do business. There is no wrong culture; it's just culture. Some cultures eat with forks, some with sticks, and others with their fingers. Is one better than the other? Not really, it's just culture and no one thinks much about what they are doing. Culture has influenced their actions and attitudes for them.

Modern culture is shaped and communicated in part by advertising. It's through these lenses that we see the shiny new cars, the latest fashions, the hottest movies, and the next "game of the century." The ads are shaping and urging us to conform to this world and to what everyone else is doing.

The next important phrase is "but be transformed." Paul wanted his readers to be changed from what they were into something new. This transformation was not going to happen through external means, but through "the renewing of your mind." The business of the mind is thinking, so Paul was pointing out that personal transformation is an internal process driven by our thoughts.

Therefore, if you are going to avoid debt addiction, which is the pattern of this world, you are going to have to think new thoughts. Before you can think new thoughts, however, you must be aware of what you are currently thinking and where those thoughts are emerging from. They sometimes come from advertising.

Ubiquitous Ads

We are bombarded with so much advertising that we often don't pay attention to its presence. We cannot access a page on the internet without an ad popping up or watch a video on YouTube without an ad interrupting it. Every inning at a baseball game or snap of a football game seems to be sponsored by someone. Ads still populate most television programs and the mail continues to produce circulars and catalogs urging us to spend some money with this company or that service. I watched a professional boxing match and the boxer advertised on his back with a tattoo for a marketing firm.

I want to start with how advertising affects debt and people who are in debt. There is a significant correlation between advertising and the increase in debt. Put simply, advertising is used to lure people into living beyond their means. If you watch TV, you see it all the time. A hamburger appears on TV and you may not be hungry or thinking hamburger, but it suggests that you leave your house and go spend money for a hamburger. Then you end up buying fries and other side orders. That's the simple power of advertising. If you don't do it when you see the ad, you may do it the next time you're out and pass that restaurant.

What's more, every time you search for something on the internet, ads begin to pop up on your Facebook page for the items you searched for. When you drive down the highway, billboards flip to another sign every few seconds, so that what was once one billboard now becomes many. All this is designed to get you to spend money, and it works. It is a coordinated effort by advertisers who are paid by those who are advertising to get you to think about and then act to purchase their products and services. These are often subliminal messages that stick with us and resonate within our minds. When your toddler or young child wants something for Christmas, they most likely saw it on TV and decided they had to have it. Be aware, there is power in targeted advertising!

Why Are They So Effective?

A good advertising hook focuses on your emotions. An effective car ad makes you feel like you are sitting in and driving the car, or makes you feel like the car you are driving is no longer worth driving. You may not go right out and purchase that car, but when the time comes, you will remember the feeling and not necessarily all the specifics about that car, or its cost. According to Amy Livingston, look out for common advertising strategies noted below.

Fear. The most powerful emotion seems to be fear. One of the easiest ways to get people to buy something is to make them fearful about *not* having that product or service. Advertisers appeal to our fear of a medical condition, being out of style, breaking down on the highway, or having our shipment not arrive on time. Therefore, the ads tell us the product or services will help us look better, live better, or work better.

Rarely if ever do we see advertisements that say to pray and trust God for what is being offered. The message is: You *must* buy this product; you *cannot* do without. Typically, credit cards are the preferred method of payment, because they guarantee you can have it now. Our fear is a significant motivating factor for advertisers because it is inherent in us as Americans who are traditionally fearful of many things, especially not having the latest and greatest of whatever we like. We are fearful of certain things, but we should not be fearful in a way that motivates us to purchase things we do not need or can't afford.

The bandwagon. Another appeal of advertising is what is called the bandwagon effect, which aims to convince us that we should do exactly what others are doing, whoever the others are. Advertisers don't broadcast their bandwagon approach, but that is what it is. Everyone else is already doing it, or purchasing it, and if you don't follow suit, you will look bad or your children or spouse won't love you. This appeal works because according to psychologists, all humans share the need to feel loved and accepted, which Abraham Maslow categorizes as a social need.

I became familiar with the writings of this psychologist in college, he developed what he refers to as "The Hierarchy of Needs." Maslow maintained that when the basic needs were met, humans would move on to fulfill the next most basic need. He identified five needs: physiological (food and clothing); safety; love, belonging; esteem; and self-actualization. The bandwagon is right in the middle of the hierarchy. We want and need to be in a community, so if everyone is driving a new car, we have a strong desire to want one too. It makes us feel like we belong.

The bandwagon effect is all about being part of something. We have to be a part of that, we have to do this, others are doing this, it's important. When we see those things in advertising, it appeals to a basic need.

Sex appeal. Advertisers use sex appeal as often as possible because sex sells. The sex drive is one of the most basic instincts humans have, even more basic than the need for love and belonging. Advertisers take full advantage of the fact that erotic images sell everything from cars to clothes. That's why today we see more advertisers using sexy models, male and female. The message is: If you wear this product or use this fragrance, you are going to look like this model who is 20 years old, even though you may be much older. The models are young, have on a lot of makeup, and have teams of people working on them so they look beautiful, but we believe if we get that product, coat, or shirt, or drive that car, we will feel good about ourselves.

That's why many movie stars have perfumes named after them. They probably don't know anything about perfumes or fragrances, but a marketer paid them to put their name on it and it sells. Because a star's name is on it, the price goes up, but people still want to buy it, often using a credit card or money that should go towards other needs.

Devastation

You still may be wondering how all this contributes to debt addiction. The same ads that sell cars and video games also sell debt. That's right, they sell you the concept that you can't live without debt (fear), everyone's using it (bandwagon), and you will be cool if you do (sex appeal). Pay attention to the ads that feature debt they use attractive stars, music and dance, or easy-to-remember slogans. There is an ad for a loan company that has a Broadway-style song and dance urging you to borrow money. If you have heard it, you'll remember it. It has a familiar tone and appeals to you so you call a 1.800 number to get your money. Devastation is what you feel when you get the bill for the purchases you made without regard for your ability to pay it back. "What am I going to do?"

Because our culture is saturated with entertainment, the ads are as entertaining as actual shows. Who doesn't watch the Big Game for the ads as well as the football? We have product spokespeople and they earnestly implore us to get up, get out, and get spending. That's why we need to have our minds renewed so we don't fall prey to the tactics of fear-producing, everyone-is-doing-it suggestions, or sexy dancing girls or muscle-bound guys.

Advertising is a means of educating the public about the products available and their features. We know that an insurance company has a product to customize your insurance quote according to your perceived needs. They have done a great job of teaching us about their products through repetitive and creative ads using a comedian as the spokesperson. She's funny, unpretentious, and seems to be doing anything but selling, but she is selling a service.

Another Example

I recently saw an ad for a reverse mortgage. I've been in the banking and housing business, so I pay attention to these ads. As a person who has been in the mortgage business, I am familiar with reverse mortgages, but you may not know what that is. The ad had a spokesperson who claimed that for someone over 60 years of age, a reverse mortgage is a good idea because the holder never has a mortgage payment again. The music was soothing, the spokesperson credible, and the concept attractive, and all that came from a 60-second spot. It could woo you to investigate, even though the product may not be the best option for you.

A reverse mortgage is when someone goes to a lending institution, and signs over their home in order to receive a monthly check based on the equity in their home. As long as a person lives in that house, they don't have to pay their mortgage. Once that person dies, however, the home is sold on the market and that is how the lender gets repaid. If they want to pass that house down to another family member, they can't do it because it is going to be sold once they pass away. Some argue it is a good product, but I don't believe it is the best product for most consumers. Remember, you never get something for nothing, and if it sounds too good to be true, it probably is.

Because advertisers know older citizens sometimes need money and live on fixed incomes, they portray the reverse mortgage as a source for peace of mind (again appealing to fear). The ad for a reverse mortgage is no different than an ad for a wristwatch, but the mortgage has more serious and long-lasting effects. The advertiser is trying to shape our values and what is important in our minds.

I sometimes see ads for renting furniture, especially around the holidays. Leasing furniture or a big-screen TV is never a good idea. The consumer may end up spending money to rent furniture at $30 a week for the next 10 years. They could have purchased that TV at some point, but instead they are renting. These are the things that cause us to get out of balance when it comes to our budget and how we manage our funds.

Before we move into a discussion of debt later in this section, I want to introduce another concept to get you thinking not only about debt reduction, but also increased income. This income can pay off debt or provide cash for you to purchase some things you want without having to resort to a credit card. As we lay the foundation for financial literacy in this section, let's look at ways to make money in the next chapter.

Chapter 3
Making Additional Money

I know you probably already have a job or other source of income, but you may not have the job you want and may not be making the money you desire or need. In order to get out of debt, you may have to find some additional revenue to help you pay off your debt. One couple sold their home, used the equity to pay off their debts, moved into an apartment for more than two years, and then bought another home. They did what they needed to do to be debt free and set free, and you also may have to do something to get there too. There are other ways to make money, so let's look at some examples that can give you some ideas.

Before I got married, I had four jobs simultaneously. I want to lay it out for you so you know it can work. You can't do this for more than two or three years, but it's possible. I was working full-time as a bank manager, a gas station attendant, in the United States Army Reserves, and at McDonald's flipping hamburgers part-time. McDonald's was three days a week, the gas station two or three evenings a week, I was full-time at the bank, and one weekend a month on duty at the U.S. Army Reserves. I had four different checks coming in every month and I needed them all.

Some Other Ways

You may be overwhelmed at the thought of having multiple jobs, so let's look at some other options too. Some people sell gently-used clothes (their own or from others), and often set up shop on eBay or one of the other online sales sites. I'm sure you may have some old clothes that you no longer wear that could be donated, but why not sell them? It's a quick way to make some money. Local consignment shops are also available to sell women's clothing. NerdWallet offers some ways below to make money.

You may have an old cell phone you can sell, along with your iPad or gaming systems that are lying around. There are sites called swappa.com and nextworth.com that you can go to as well. Also, check out Amazon's trade-in program that pays participants with gift cards. If you are in need of cash, try ecoATM. These are things that don't take a lot of time but can be effective. (And if you are not tech savvy, then find a young person to help you set things up.)

You can rent out your parking spot, which in some locales can be a hot commodity, particularly in urban, densely-populated areas. Some people have driveways with spaces they don't use. They can rent them out through Craigslist or through other services.

How about driving for Uber or Lyft, or both? A lot of people are doing that and they're bringing home a lot of extra money. Another way is making deliveries for Amazon, Ubereats, Instakcrat, Postmates, or Amazon Flex. You get paid to make deliveries and in most cases, you can even earn tips. A car is not always required either. Postmark allows you to use a bicycle, scooter, or your own two feet to make deliveries. That's another interesting way to earn money.

Another way to earn cash is to pick up freelance work from websites like Upwork, Fiver, and Freelancer. Those sites offer freelance jobs like writing, programming, design, marketing, data entry, or being a virtual assistant. There's another good source referred to as testing websites and apps like usertesting.com. That site will pay you for your thoughts about how well or not so well certain websites and apps work. You will have to pass a test to be accepted, and then you'll be paid $10 for each 20-minute test that involves recording and answering four follow-up questions.

You can pick up tasks on Amazon Mechanical Touch as well. Even in the age of automation and technology, some jobs still require a human touch. Companies often outsource these jobs to services like AmazonTurk. These jobs can be tedious, things like tagging images, transcribing videos, calling, and transcribing receipts, and can take anywhere from a few minutes to a few hours. The pay depends on the task and the person requesting the work must approve the finished product before you get paid.

How about renting out your spare room or even your home through AirBnB? If you enjoy putting together Ikea furniture or standing in a long line, you could be called up to do tasks for others. Taskrabbit can connect you to people who need help with a variety of things, like moving, cleaning, deliveries, or being a handyman. You can make money from your blogs. If you are a blogger you can make money through your site traffic.

More Money or More Debt?

Where am I going with all this? I want you to realize that you don't have to rely on credit to increase or supplement your income. Often people get cash advances from their cards because they need money, but you have to pay a fee to get the cash and then pay interest on what you borrowed. If you are going to spend money, then look for ways to make money and not use credit. Also, don't diminish the importance of paying more than your minimum payment on any debt you have. It adds up over time and will help reduce interest owed. If you can bring in $180 a month in extra income, let that be the money you spend to quickly pay down your debt. Discipline yourself to restrict spending to what you have, not what you can borrow, even if you can make the payments.

An effective budget comes down to knowing what you have coming in and then what you can spend and the discipline to stick with it. We will discuss budgeting a little later, but I want to encourage you now to search for some additional resources through the ideas I have given you. Spend some time brainstorming with your family (how about childcare or sitting with the elderly?), and have fun seeing how much more revenue you can generate, not just so you can spend, but so you can save and get out of debt.

Now you understand that you are constantly barraged with messages to spend more, and the temptation is there to use credit cards to do so. Instead, think about how you can enhance your revenue or income stream. As you do that, you should be aware of what is often the largest debt payment you have, which is your mortgage. As you will learn in the next chapter, paying that off can be a tremendous source of freedom and available cash for you to save or spend.

"Because financially capable consumers ultimately contribute to a stable economic and financial system, as well as, improve their own financial situations; it's clear that the Federal Reserve has a significant stake in financial education."
- Ben Bernanke

Chapter 4
Mortgage Smarts

The mortgage payment is the first line of attack to be debt free and set free, and it's often a consumer's highest single payment. My wife and I paid off our home mortgage in just 14 years. Our house payment was the largest liability we had at the time and it took a concerted effort to do so. Since this is a section on financial literacy, let's make sure you understand what goes into a mortgage and why it's in your best interest to pay it off early.

There are four components to a mortgage payment: principal, interest, taxes, and insurance. The principal portion is the amount that pays down your outstanding balance. Interest is the cost of borrowing the money and the amount of interest you pay is determined by your interest rate and loan balance. The principal is the actual amount of the loan you pay interest on to the bank. If you buy a $100,000 home and put $10,000 down, then you have a monthly payment to pay back the $90,000 you borrowed, that is the principal. If you pay off the principal ahead of schedule, which you are permitted to do, you can save tens of thousands of dollars in interest payments. While paying off the principal takes money out of your budget initially, it will eventually put a lot of money back into your monthly budget.

Pay It Off Early

If that does not compel you to pay off the mortgage early, think about this: You may be paying as much as 69.5% of your original mortgage amount in interest if you keep the mortgage for 30 years (that's enough to purchase a second home as an investment property). Who would you rather have get the money you save from paying the mortgage off early, you or the lender? In today's economy, having this money can be invested or used for retirement. With a mortgage loan amount of $136,000 at 6% interest for 30 years, you will pay $293,540.00 in total, which includes $157,540.07 in interest payments.

Here's how you pay off your mortgage early. It requires discipline and minimizing other debt, so all your excess cash can be used to pay on the mortgage. Using the same example, here is the plan. Depending on how quickly you want to pay your mortgage off determines how much more you pay monthly. Here is the model we used to pay our house off in 14 years. Using an average loan amount of $136,000, the payment for 30 years at 6% would be $815. Divide the payment in half, which equals $407.50. Add that amount to your monthly payment, which would total $1,222.50.

If you made the extra $407.50 per month at the start of your mortgage, you will pay the loan off in 13.5 years (less than half the time of the original mortgage) and you would be saving $94,782.00. You could do less than half your payment if that's too much. Try dividing the monthly payment by three, which equals $271.66 for a total monthly payment of $1,087.18. Then you would pay the loan off in 16.3 years, saving $78,564. You can customize an amortization schedule by going to www.financial-calculators.com/amortization-schedule. You may wonder where you would get the extra to add to your monthly payment, but you have it right now in the credit card payments you are making. When you eliminate those payments, you are also eliminating the exorbitant interest payments of up to 18 percent.

According to a study by the Federal Reserve Bank, 43 percent of American families spend more money than they earn on an annual basis, and the average household carries about $8,000 in credit card debt. I just figured it out for you; eliminating the credit card debt gives you even more than the $407.69 a month to pay off the loan in just 13.5 years.

Therefore, stop using the cards because they cost you too much (see the chapter on credit cards). I repeat that according to the Federal Reserve, 43 percent of American families spend more money than they earn on an annual basis. To do this consciously or subconsciously borders on illogical (for the educated); indifference (for the intellectuals); ridiculous (for the unimpressed); foolish (for the fools); unbiblical (for the Christians); a fumble (for the athletes); a closed caucus (for the politicians); and not pretty (for the good-looking). For the automobile industry, however, it sounds perfectly normal as long as you purchase a car. You will not be set free if you continue to spend more than you earn. And once you become a homeowner, you'll need additional cash to maintain the house and to augment any downward trend in your home equity that most homeowners expect to gain over time.

Other Factors

As you consider the actual purchase of a home, there are many factors that come into play, such as how much house can you afford? Is there a good chance the house will appreciate in value? Is the house in a stable community? What is the school district like (if you have children still in school)? Is it close to a shopping area? Hospital? Major highway?

There are several factors that can determine the percentage of your monthly budget that should go to housing. Many potential homeowners think just of the mortgage payment itself when considering purchasing a home, but there is much more to consider (and budget for) when looking to become a homeowner. Below is a basic list of items you should budget for, inclusive of the monthly mortgage payment, to capture the real cost of what the home you are considering will cost:

- Mortgage payment
- Mortgage insurance (with less than 20% down private mortgage insurance)
- Monthly real estate taxes
- Electricity, gas, water
- Phone, cable TV, and internet
- Maintenance

Lenders use debt-to-income (DTI) ratios to determine how much of your gross income is going towards paying debts. DTIs often cover more than just debts and can include principal, taxes, fees, and insurance premiums as well. There are two kinds of debt-to-income ratios: the front ratio and back-end ratio, stated as 28/36.

1. The front-end ratio indicates the percentage of income that goes toward housing costs, which for renters is the rent amount and for homeowners is the principal, interest, taxes, and insurance.
2. The second DTI, known as the back-end ratio, indicates the percentage of income that goes toward paying all debt payments,

including those covered by the first DTI, and other debts such as credit cards, a car loan, student loans, child support, alimony, and legal judgments. Utility payments are not included in the DTI ratios.

If the lender requires a debt-to-income ratio of 28/36 to qualify a borrower for a mortgage, the lender generally goes through the following process to determine what expense levels are acceptable for their particular bank or lending institution. This may vary by lender.

- Using a sample salary on an annualized basis:
  - Gross Income of $58,000
  - $58,000 x 28% = $16,240 allowed for housing expense annually
  - $58,000 x 36% = $20,880 allowed for housing expense and recurring debt annually
- Using the same sample salary, but on a monthly basis:
  - Gross Income of $4,833.33 ($58,000 over 12 months)
  - $4,833.33 x 28% = $1,353.33 allowed for housing expense.
  - $4,833.33 x 36% = $1,739.99 allowed for housing expense plus recurring debt.

While utilities and cable TV are not part of the actual mortgage payment, they are tied to the home and should be included. These expenses vary every month, and they depend on a home's energy efficiency and how the owner manages these costs (for example, at what temperature will you set your thermostat?). Of all the budget categories families have, the housing-expense category is the largest percentage of a household's annual budget in most cases (we will discuss budgeting later).

It is sad that individuals, who spend 15 or 20 years paying a mortgage can still end up losing their home because they owe another 10 years and are unable to pay due to unforeseen circumstances or poor financial choices. Let's return to the example of a mortgage of $136,000 at 6% for 30 years with a monthly payment of $815.00. After paying for 20 years, you have paid $195,600.60 on the home, only to lose it. This is what has happened to many Americans today, and often it's not due to their unwillingness to pay. There are many reasons for paying off your mortgage sooner rather than later, which not only includes the first mortgage, but other debt that may be collateralized by the home, such as a home equity loan. Even the no-money down refinancing should be thoroughly vetted before signing on the dotted line. These products just keep your debt alive under the guise of helping you.

Losing a House

Each year you still owe on your home exposes you to the possibility of losing your home. There are thousands over the past five years who never thought they would lose their largest investment, but they did. Paying off the mortgage early is not just about money saved, but about protecting your largest asset in most cases, otherwise known as being set free. Because this is usually the largest debt people owe, there is an anxiety that comes with owing hundreds of thousands of dollars. The pressure homeowners experience is real and continuous. No matter the circumstances, those who owe mortgage debt often unconsciously think about it, not to mention the other side of how you furnish, maintain the upkeep, and pay the taxes and utilities. This is the reason I appeal to you to do what you must to experience the blessing that comes with making that last mortgage payment years early.

You must make sure you annotate when making principal payments and differentiate them from the regular monthly mortgage payment. When it's time to pay the mortgage off, you must be intentional with the lender so what you want gets done. When we paid our mortgage, we kept getting charged small interest payments even though we paid the amount to cover multiple payments. We ultimately made a final large principle payment, which exceeded the balance and interest owed, thereby causing the lender to send us the difference back.

There are many theories on the benefits of paying off a mortgage early or not, but if you read the Bible, there is a verse that sums it up quite well: "The rich ruleth over the poor, and the borrower is servant to the lender" (Proverbs 22:7). This is one of the most profound passages in the Bible regarding being a borrower. If the Bible deals with this issue forthrightly, shouldn't you?

Some individuals who have worked and earned money for 40 years eventually retire, but then need to find a job, not because they want to work, but because they still have so much debt. How can you still owe money on your house if you had a 30-year mortgage 40 years ago? It's possible because you had two refinances, a home equity loan, and late payments throughout the term of the loan. If you ever took the time to closely review the amortization schedule, you would see that the cost of refinancing may not be beneficial in the long term despite the immediate reduction of the mortgage payment.

This simply means you pay less on the principal of the mortgage each month, which means you will be in debt even longer and pay more in interest. Don't forget, you are supposed to save or invest the savings, but perhaps you refinanced because you could not afford the mortgage in the first place. If you must refinance a mortgage, and ultimately pay thousands more over time just to save $100.00 per month or so, you really can't afford the mortgage. Not only can't you afford it, you are going further in debt, so you can expect to be strapped with this mortgage, which will ultimately cause you to have more stress, maybe be late on other loans, and all for what?

Ask questions, pray, and be smart before you make these supposedly good decisions. The lenders are not in business to make things better for you. They are in business to make money. How are you going to be free of debt, when you let debt be your friend and hang out with you all year long? Read Psalm 112:3, which says, "Wealth and riches shall be in his house; and his righteousness endureth for ever." The Word of God is true and everlasting, and the Bible also says in James 2:17 "Even so faith, if it hath not works, is dead, being alone."

After a house, what else does almost every household need one of, and maybe more than one? It is an automobile, which can be the next biggest expense in a household budget. Let's turn our attention to that topic as we continue to expand the scope of your financial literacy.

Chapter 5
Buying Four Wheels

To gain wealth, you have to work at it. It won't happen by osmosis or hoping. You have to exhibit both faith *and* works. Many Christians have faith, but their works where finances are concerned sometimes is lacking. Many have great faith in the areas of healing, finding a spouse, or faith for the needs of others. They believe God will deliver them or their family members from long prison sentences or drugs or serious illness, but when it comes to faith to gain wealth is sometimes non-existent. Why have great faith in so many other areas, but limited faith when it comes to finances? Gaining wealth requires the denial of pleasure, the holding back on that car you want even if you can afford it and believe you deserve it. Buying four wheels can have consequences.

At one time, I owned a luxury vehicle, but I purchased the car used. I let someone else pay the luxury tax. I negotiated well after waiting nearly four months to get the car. I went to the dealership every month to see if the car was still there. It was winter in Pittsburgh, so snow covered the car. It sat all winter, meaning the price continually dropped (there is a right time to purchase any vehicle).

I studied this process, all the while saving the money I had because I had no car payment for years. I previously owned an Infiniti Q-45 for eight years, and saved the money every month that would have been my car payment, which allowed me to have enough money to put down on my next car. Having cash, knowing how long the car sat on their lot, purchasing it before the weather changed to warm weather, and waiting until the end of the month, all contributed to a deal in my favor. I learned early in life always to be prepared to walk away from any deal, no matter how badly I wanted it.

When purchasing a car, use your savings, buy smart, and if you must have a payment, always pay the car off in 24 months or less. This is how you minimize paying a lot of money on a depreciating asset. When you buy a two-year-old car and pay it off in two years, it may still have some value, but most importantly, you own it and it's only four years old. *Consumer Reports* (www.consumerreports.org) says "the average life expectancy of a new vehicle is around eight years or 150,000 miles. Of course, some well-built vehicles can go 15 years and 300,000 if properly maintained."

Buying Smart

Vehicle purchases are a decision most people have to make. Some individuals have made bad choices and then are stuck with a negative-equity dilemma. As a former bank manager, I have witnessed the effects of this firsthand and you should be aware of it. If you are, you should ensure your siblings, children, and friends know how to avoid this situation. In some cases, an individual wants to purchase a vehicle and, due to financial circumstances, they may not be in a position at the time to purchase a suitable car with the necessary coverages for maintenance and other rudimentary damages and coverage items.

Let's say a person walks into a dealership or a roadside shop and purchases a ten-year old jalopy. It runs, but it could also break down in the next five minutes. Due to limited funds, however, they purchase this car and pay more than what it's worth because there are no credit checks. They need to pay $4,000, which is $1,500 above the value of the car. It did well for the first year, but then they are back at the dealer with a car that does not run. Even though they made every payment, they still owe $1,500 and are looking for another car.

Now, if you want to be set free to become debt free, never take the amount you owe from the first car and add it to the new balance on the next car. Even if you can afford the higher payments (you've just been victimized), you can be in a negative-equity position as a result of this decision. Now you owe more money on a depreciating asset, and it's rare you will ever catch up, which is where my old bank collection days come into play.

It's called repossession by the repo man.

When I was in the collection department for the bank, we thrived on repossessing cars, particularly when individuals tried to play the game of hide and seek. The borrower would always lose the car, still owe the money, and then had negative credit, no wheels, and they still owed the difference between what the bank could sell the car for and the remaining balance they owed. They still owed that and it can and will appear on their credit report.

Remember, this all started with purchasing a car that was junk. You paid too much, rolled it over to a newer car, which you could not maintain. The bank still got paid and the collection department got a bonus based on how well it did collecting the money you owed the bank. I was good at it, but I was always fair.

Nonetheless, there were times when our group wanted to reach someone because they called and either were deceptive over the phone or they were a skip-trace, meaning we could not find them because they were allusive. Sometimes we had the client on the phone and they lied about who they were, saying they were a brother or cousin. If you play games with the lenders, you only make it more difficult for yourself. Always be proactive when you know you are past due or going to be past due, and tell the bank or lender. You will receive well-structured treatment, especially when collateral is involved. Why do you think the banks require collateral in the first place? They can take your collateral in lieu of payment when you default and they will.

I could share many stories from my days as a bank collector. There was a gentleman who was past due on his car note but was always one step ahead of our repossession team, until once when he and his girlfriend went to a restaurant to eat. Remember, repossession is a 24/7 business and can occur anywhere (other than on your premises) or at any time. Can you imagine how this individual felt when he came out of the restaurant with his date only to see his car being hoisted on a flatbed truck and being taken away? There was no way to adequately explain this to his girlfriend who he was trying to impress. Stories like that happened all the time.

Negative Net Worth

In the introduction, I mentioned that it is possible to have a negative net worth if you don't manage your debt carefully. I also promised an explanation of how that can happen, so here it is.

An individual purchased a vehicle that was seven years old, paid $4,000 for the car even though at the time the car was valued at $3,000.

It ran well, looked good, and at the time met the needs of the purchaser. Because the car was seven years old, it depreciated significantly and one year later, it was only worth $1,500. Within two years, the car broke down, and the borrower still owed $1,800 on the car. It would have cost $900 to repair the engine, so the borrower was stuck with a car that had a balance due of $1,800. The borrower was still in need of a vehicle that is operable and reliable, but could not afford the cost to repair it, meaning they needed $900 cash, plus continuing the payments on the car.

Here's where the negative equity begins and it happens frequently. Since the borrower could not come up with the $900, they went back to the same car dealer, who was all too happy to see the customer back in the dealership. I guess you know what happened before I tell you: The borrower walked out with another used car and the dealer simply added the additional $1,800 they owed on the previous car to the balance of the new used car. This had progressed into what I call negative equity, the debt owed exceeded the value of the vehicle, thereby causing negative equity.

Even if the borrower attempted to sell the just-purchased car, it's at least $1,800 more than the value of the car is and it will only get worse as the car rapidly depreciates, causing the negative equity to grow even faster. If this borrower has no other credit, when a creditor reviews their credit report, they will see a car balance higher than the value of the car (negative equity). This person can ultimately get back to positive equity, but it will require paying off the car, and not refinancing the remaining balance for another car purchase.

Remember, advertising is working hard to shape your values, especially where a car purchase is concerned. Those ads tell you how much you can save if you buy now, but they don't really tell you how much you will spend if you finance the car. Take your time, do the research, seek advice from those you trust (not the salesperson, who may be trustworthy, but has a job to do and that is to sell you a car), and buy smart. If you can do that, then you are ready for the next lesson in financial literacy and that is how to manage those little pieces of plastic called credit cards. Let's go there now.

Chapter 6
Credit Card Debt

Credit cards are used frequently today by more Americans (and citizens of the world) than ever before. The statistics are mind boggling, but here they are:

1. 261 million VISA cards
2. 176 million MasterCards
3. 50.6 million American Express cards

I am willing to say that you are numbered among these statistics.

Credit cards are by nature unsecured, which means the lending institution extends credit to you based on your promise to pay it back. They cannot repossess things you bought with your card, like they can with a car or house loan. With that in mind, I can tell you that some of the unsecured credit limits are higher than the average cost to purchase a home and this is not relegated to high-wealth income individuals, but high-credit-worthy individuals too.

It's the use and nonpayment of credit cards that can singlehandedly destroy your credit and keep you in debt for years. If you ever expect to be debt free, you must begin with being credit-card-less. That does not mean you should not have a credit, charge, or debit card, you will need one to rent a car, book a hotel or airline tickets, and things of this sort. It's how effectively you manage the use of the card that will be an indicator of your addiction to debt. Bank credit card delinquencies are at a 15-year low as of the third quarter of 2016, according to the American Bankers Association Consumer Credit Delinquency survey below.

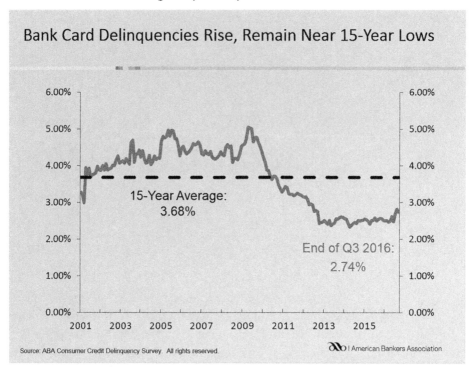

Bank Card Delinquencies Rise, Remain Near 15-Year Lows

15-Year Average: 3.68%

End of Q3 2016: 2.74%

ABA | American Bankers Association

According to www.creditcards.com, "American's revolving debt total is $1.027 trillion as of March 2018, the bulk of which is credit card debt." Not paying on time complicates the problem of becoming debt free. Many individuals believe that paying late on a credit card, particularly when the monthly payment is relatively small (say $48), does not matter. Any late payment, no matter how small it is, can cause your credit score to drop and the balance due can grow until you are in over your head.

One missed payment of $48 can not only prevent you from securing credit and drop your credit score, but you also pick up late fees and interest, which add up quickly. Many credit card fees can be as high as $30 for a late payment or an over-the-limit payment. You owed $48 and suddenly you owe $78, and if you then pay the minimum payment of $2 (3%), you still have a balance, and the cycle continues. Now multiply that times five different credit cards and you can see what a nightmare credit cards can be if you are not on top of the situation.

The average credit card debt according to www.creditcard.com is:

- $1,154 per card that doesn't carry a balance
- $1,734 per account for U.S. adults with a credit report and social security number
- $1,841 average balance on store credit cards
- $4,087 per person U.S. resident
- $5.422 per cardholder, excluding unused and store cards
- $5.839 per U.S. adult with a credit card
- $6,354 average balance on credit cards at the end of 2017

According to a Time/CNN article dated May, 12, 2009 written by Barbara Kivist, "There are piles of evidence that people are bad decision makers when it comes to how they use credit cards. Even when presented with full and fair information, they often make decisions that are not in their own economic best interest."

Credit card companies rely on Americans to be lackadaisical in their decision making and that's why they offer teaser (lower-appearing) rates to get people using their card. You should not choose to use a card based on its short-term teaser rate. In all likelihood, even with good intentions, you will owe more because the discipline needed to pay cards off in full monthly, or even on time, alludes many card holders. Then when the card's rate increases after a period of time, you will find yourself locked into a high rate of interest. The article further stated,

> "Certain economists, though, have another way of looking at that and similar findings. They see a systematic psychological breakdown, as a species we're just really bad at understanding costs that comes later on. Instead, we assign a disproportionate amount of importance to what's immediate and tangible. We lock eyes with that initial low rate and can't look away" (And, yes, credit-card companies get that). "It gets worse, in one experiment, Drazen Prelec and Duncan Simester of the Massachusetts Institute of Technology found that people were willing to pay twice as much for basketball tickets when they were using a credit card as opposed to paying cash. Credit-card spending just doesn't feel like real money."

In another study, Nicholas Souleles of the University of Pennsylvania and David Gross of the consultancy, Compass Lexicon calculated that the typical consumer unnecessarily spends $200 every year in interest payments by keeping a sizable stash of cash in savings or checking while at the same time carrying a credit card balance. The aforementioned statements are exactly what I mean when I say that when you become debt free, you are set free. There is an emotional and physiological effect that people go through when they have debt, even a little debt, it's a constant concern. What happens if I can't pay the debt? Will I ever come out of this? People feel this way for years, and that will have an impact on them over time, even if they subconsciously believe it won't. At some point, you know you've thought, "I'll never get out of this situation," and the mood grows more somber and dark, sometimes resulting in depression.

This problem can be masked well, but not internally, which is why you have to deal with it by changing your situation. If you don't deal with it, it will deal with you. In 2007, the Time/CNN article stated, a group of senators introduced a bill that required credit card companies to state on each billing statement how long it would take a person to pay off the balance and how much it would cost in principal and interest should they make only the minimum required payment each month. (That's another psychological trip-up: having a low minimum payment printed on the statement in a big font changes our perception of how much we should be paying off, and can mean we carry higher balances for longer). Do not be fooled by these designs.

Easy to Get In, Hard to Get Out

I can't emphasize enough that credit card debt is the easiest debt to get into, and the hardest to get out of, simply because of the ease of entry. When no collateral is required, and limits are as low as $200.00, it's a disaster recipe for the borrowing novice or the financially illiterate. That may sound tough, but that's what you are when you dabble in borrowing and have no clue what you are doing, or far worse, no plan to get out of debt.

According to a recent survey conducted by the National Association for Business Economics (www.nabe.com),

> The combined threat of subprime loan defaults and excessive indebtedness has overtaken terrorism and the Middle East as the biggest short-term threat to the U.S. economy. Thirty-two percent of the survey participants cited loan defaults and excessive debt as the biggest threat, compared to only 20% citing terrorism as the biggest threat.

Think about that. The threat of debt has surpassed the concern for terrorism in the Middle East. That's why being set free is vitally important, when debt is a problem greater than terrorism, to some. The pressure, challenges, and late nights dreaming about what you are going to say when the bill collectors call can be life threatening. You become afraid to answer the phone, you want to be honest, but are conflicted about how you remain honest, after you go another month without paying the bills, which can become an ongoing problem.

You choose to ignore the problem, and continue to go to restaurants, even if it's a fast-food chain that may cost you and your family $50. That may not seem like much, but any expense when you are unable to pay your bills is too much. You continue to be bound and addicted as you order the food, pay for the movie tickets, or buy that new suit, even though you know you can't afford it. The power of spending is so strong and the addiction so intense that you are unable to stop yourself from pushing the credit card in the card reader and waiting for an acceptance beep. You have no cash, but the plastic is like a drug. You've got to have it or you'll go crazy, all the while knowing it's bad for you. Why do you keep doing this to yourself and family while setting a poor example for future generations?

A National Association for Business Economics report stated,

> "Sixty-four percent of the people polled who carry debt admitted that debt is a cause of worry for them. The study also found that men worry less than women about the debt they carry. Americans have conflicting attitudes about debt. Seventy-two percent believe that debt is a part of modern life and difficult to avoid." (Source: *Don't Get Clobbered by Credit Cards* from www.parade.com and garyweiss.blogspot.com).

With credit cards, the statistics show consumers are paying higher interest rates that are unprecedented. Even with the rate teasers to get you started, consumers are making irresponsible credit card choices.

Having good credit is one of the main factors in getting insurance or even maybe a job. Your FICO score is what lenders review prior to offering you credit. The allure of being approved for credit is so strong that you will take any rate offered, just so you can spend more money, thus paying the credit card company more interest. In reality, the item(s) you purchase with the card are non-appreciating assets, things like designer clothes or other non-essential items that keep you addicted. It's like putting yourself in prison and throwing away the key. As ridiculous as that sounds, that's what you are doing when you take the card, spend, spend, and spend, while being unconcerned with the interest rate or how long it will take you to pay it off. Six months later you may not remember what you purchased. The average credit card interest rate is 19.05% for new credit card offers and 13.08% for existing accounts, according to WalletHub's 2018 *Credit Card Landscape* report (www.wallethub.com/edu/average-credit-card-interest-rate/50841/).

Now think about this. Multiply 19% by ten credit cards with the average balance on each of $9,840 which is based on the statistic that "At least 14% of the U.S. population has 10 credit cards in their wallets" (Experian's National Score Index). Therefore, if you are that one-in-ten person, then on average you owe $98,400 in credit card debt alone. You also are paying 19% on the debt or approximately $18,696 annually in interest. That is enough to purchase a new car with cash each year you have that amount of debt.

It's also true that if you frequently use credit cards, you could not tell a friend or show what you purchased with the credit cards a year after the purchase. It's foolish to just waste money, particularly when you don't often benefit long term from the purchases you've made. Today, you can use your credit cards nearly anywhere and while the ease of credit card use was supposed to make it more convenient for you, it put you into more debt.

Not only that, "Approximately half of all credit card holders don't pay the full amount of credit card charges each month. About 11% say they usually pay only the minimum monthly payment, but not much more" (Experian-Gallup Personal Credit Index survey). Not paying more than the monthly balance can often mean you will owe the credit card companies money for years, so don't expect to be set free or debt free if you keep playing with the fire of credit cards.

If you are facing the reality of your credit card problem, here are some things to keep in mind, such as your rights and the credit card company's forbidden practices as a result of the CARD Act.

- The credit card company cannot charge an inactivity fee.
- When a charge exceeds the account's credit line, an over-the-limit fee of more than the amount charged cannot be assessed.
- Consumers can no longer be charged multiple penalty fees for the same transaction. Both a late fee and an over-limit fee resulting from the same transaction cannot be charged.
- The credit card company cannot assess a late fee of more than $25 unless one of the consumer's last six payments was late, in which case the fee may go up to $35. However, if the credit card company can demonstrate that the costs it incurred as a result of the late payments justified a higher-fee, they are allowed to impose a higher penalty.
- The credit card company cannot charge a late payment fee that is more than the minimum payment.

- The company must explain any increase in the card's annual percentage rate (APR).
- If the APR is increased, the companies must re-evaluate every six months and if appropriate, reduce the rate within 45 days after completing the evaluation.

The Racial Wealth Gap Remains

Here is a short quiz that was in a New York Times article dated September 18, 2017 titled "Whites Have Huge Wealth Edge Over Blacks (But Don't Know It)." See how well you do with your answers (answers are at the end of this chapter):

1. For every $100 earned by an average white family, how much do you think is earned by an average black family? A) $0–$25; B) $26–$50; C) $51–$75; D) $76–$100; E) $100+
2. For every $100 in wealth accumulated by an average white family, how much wealth has the average black family accumulated? A) $0–$25; B) $26–$50; C) $51–$75; D) $76–$100: E) $100+

Especially for minorities, it is imperative that we take every opportunity to improve our net worth, eliminate debt, and save earnestly. At no time in American history have minorities exceeded or been on par with higher-earning income groups. Minorities still lag far behind other groups and the only way this will change is if minorities change the way we handle money. While there are still some inequities, don't wait in the hope that this will change, although it should and we pray that it does. In the meantime, do what you can do and control what you can control. There is nothing preventing any group of people from being free of debt, which is a choice every individual can make and achieve.

A family may not have the net worth or assets they have hoped for at a certain point in their lives, but having no debt is a far better scenario than having lots of it. Moreover, without debt, it is easier to amass wealth because quite simply, you have no debt so you can save and pay cash for items you want or need. This is the reason my book is not about how to gain wealth, but rather about the reasons and means to eliminate the debt burden in your life. The next page has some data that demonstrates the vast difference in wealth and income among various groups. While it is a dismal account of where we are, it should also make you realize when comparing groups that if you don't change how you handle money and eliminate debt, you'll remain in the unsettling statistical account cited below in an article written by Kimberly Amadeo (December 11, 2018, www.thebalance.com):

"The racial wealth gap in the United States is the disparity in median household wealth between the different races. This gap is most pronounced between white households and racial minorities. Whites have more wealth than black, Latino, and Native-American households. A 2018 survey found that whites severely underestimate the racial wealth gap. They think that black wealth is about 80 percent that of whites. Data from the U.S. Census Bureau reveals that black wealth is about 7 percent that of whites. In 2014, the median net worth of non-Hispanic white households was $130,800. The median net worth of black households was $9,590. It was $17,5300 for Hispanic households. Native American wealth has not even been measured since 2000. At that time, their median household net worth was just $5,700.

In like contrast, Asian American households have more wealth than white households. The richest Asian Americans held 168 times more wealth than the poorest Asian Americans. It's a greater disparity that white households, where the richest 10 percent owned 121 times more than the poorest 10 percent. The gap is worsening. Between 1983 and 2013, white households saw their wealth increase *by* 14 percent. But during the same period, black household wealth declined 75 percent. Median Hispanic household wealth declined 50 percent.

One reason for the discrepancy is the number of extremely poor black families. The Economic Policy Institute reported that 25 percent of black households have zero or negative net worth. Only 10 percent of white families are that poor. Since so many black families own nothing or are in debt, it drags down average wealth for the entire race. As a result, black families have $5.04 in net worth for every $100 held by white families. This racial wealth gap exists even among blacks who are highly educated and come from two-parent homes. Black families with graduate or professional degrees have $200,000 less in wealth than similarly-educated whites. These black or Latino college graduates don't even have as much wealth as white high school dropouts. Similarly, two-parent black households have less wealth than single-parent white households."

On the following pages are two charts that further depict the U.S. racial gap in wealth.

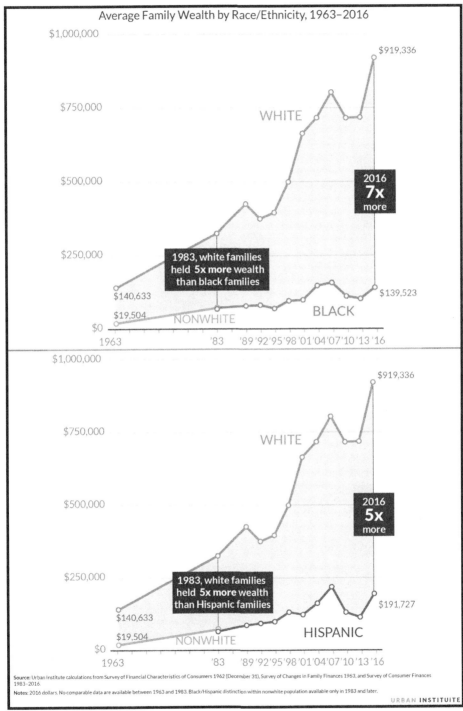

Average Family Wealth by Race/Ethnicity, 1963–2016

Source: Urban Institute calculations from Survey of Financial Characteristics of Consumers 1962 (December 31), Survey of Changes in Family Finances 1963, and Survey of Consumer Finances 1983-2016.

Notes: 2016 dollars. No comparable data are available between 1963 and 1983. Black/Hispanic distinction within nonwhite population available only in 1983 and later.

URBAN **INSTITUITE**

The racial wealth gap is real in America and there are companies who understand the importance of equal pay. There are many companies

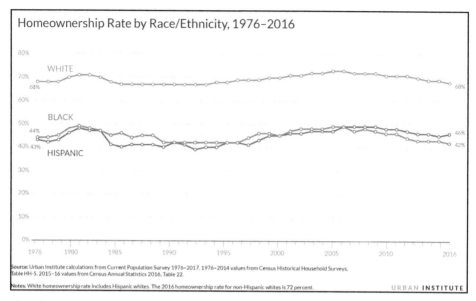

Homeownership Rate by Race/Ethnicity, 1976–2016

Source: Urban Institute calculations from Current Population Survey 1976–2017. 1976–2014 values from Census Historical Household Surveys, Table HH-5. 2015–16 values from Census Annual Statistics 2016, Table 22.

Notes: White homeownership rate includes Hispanic whites. The 2016 homeownership rate for non-Hispanic whites is 72 percent.

URBAN INSTITUTE

that have not yet made a concerted effort to minimize disparities in pay. While pay is not the only factor that results in more or less wealth, it's certainly at the top end of the spectrum that can lead to greater wealth and minimize wealth inequality. Because the wealth gap is so large, it's also incumbent on consumers to recognize they are ultimately responsible for their ability to accumulate wealth despite these disparities.

This means making smarter purchases, particularly on items that appreciate, not on those that depreciate. It also means saving more and eating out less, while also seeking jobs that pay better or more equitably. The racial wealth gap is not new and has remained intact for many years. While change is inevitable, it will not happen quickly, which is even more of a reason why you should not get addicted to debt. By remaining in debt, in addition to the racial wealth gap if it applies to you, it will take a longer time to grow your assets and increase your net worth.

My wife and I began to save money early in our marriage and you should too, even though it may not be at the level you want. Starting a serious savings plan is critical to experiencing the debt-free life (more on savings in a later chapter). It takes discipline and a commitment to stay on track with a good savings plan. The expectation is that you will achieve your goal if you stick with it. It's imperative for you to understand that if you do not achieve your goal, no matter how great the racial wealth gap is and despite the fact that you did not get the job (or pay) you wanted, you cannot blame anyone else. No one other than you is responsible for staying out of debt and increasing your net worth.

Your inaction will result in an element of unpredictability and lack of fulfillment in your financial life. If in 10, 15, or 20 years you are no further along with income, savings, and net worth achievements than you are now, whose fault is it really? According to the Racial Wealth Gap study, the three main factors driving the income gap between white, black, and hhispanic households are homeownership, education, and labor markets. The typical while family earns $50,400; the typical Latino family earns $36,840; and the typical black family earns $32,038. You should first make a commitment to follow the principles I am advocating to become debt free. The challenge is that income equality has yet to translate into wealth equality and economic security for black or Latino households.

The financial dilemma that Americans face is not new, but consistently repetitive. Americans say they want to be in control of their financial destiny, but like preparing for a boxing match, they don't want to do the training to prepare for the match. Without putting the work in before stepping into the ring, the likelihood of winning is zilch. In the financial arena, unprepared means remaining in debt.

A large number of Americans have relied for years on the federal government to provide housing and food-stamps, Social Security, disability income, and other forms of government assistance. For legitimate reasons, government help is appropriate and may be necessary, and I understand that all too well. My Godly mother at one time in her life temporarily received welfare, but went on to earn an associate's degree and bachelor of science degree from the University of Pittsburgh. After that, she worked for more than twenty years as a counselor in the Pittsburgh Public School system from where she retired.

If you need assistance, just don't get too comfortable and complacent, or become reliant on government assistance. It was designed to be temporary, not permanent, and more importantly, it is unlikely you will gain wealth and accumulate tangible assets that can be passed on to children and grandchildren based solely on government assistance. I wrote this book to specifically encourage and tell you that you can live debt free and increase your net worth, no matter what the statistics say. It's clearly stated in Proverbs 22:7, which says, "The rich ruleth over the poor and the borrower is servant to the lender." If you are the poor or the borrower, that's not where you want to remain. It might be where you are now or have been (I have been a borrower), but just don't stay there. Change does not happen by osmosis, so you have to do something; so do something!

One way that minorities have worked to close the wealth and income gap in the United States is through higher education. People pursuing more education, however often go into debt to finance their schooling, and this has created another source of debt that has reached staggering proportions. Let's look at the concept of student loans in the next chapter.

Answer to question 1: Black families in America earn $57.30 for every $100 in white-family income.

Answer to question 2: For every $100 in white-family wealth, black families hold $5.04.

Chapter 7
Student Loans

Studies reveal that only 39% of Americans have enough savings to cover a $1,000 emergency today, so the concept of saving for a college education is foreign to them. If you want to earn an education by attending college or trade school, many citizens typically seek out student loans for themselves or their children. There is an epidemic in the way student loans are being managed. Student loan debt exceeded credit card debt in 2010 and car loan debt in 2011 and exceeded the one trillion-dollar mark in 2016 and is still growing

In 2016, more than two-thirds of college graduates had average debt upon graduation of about $35,000, tripling in the last two decades. Student loan debt is increasing because government grants and support for post-secondary education failed to keep pace with the increases in college costs, whether it is a smaller college, public or private school. Therefore, the student loan crisis in many cases is worse than what the average person has been led to believe.

When I was a bank manager years ago, we had mothers and fathers who came in to borrow money against their home to provide money for their kids to go to college. Now that is certainly feasible if you can manage that. In one case, however, the child never finished college. Therefore, the parents had debt on their house but because the son did not graduate, he was unable to pay his parents back, which became a significant problem for them.

They were relying on him to graduate and pay it back because they could not get a deferment on the payments for a home equity loan like on a student loan. The second mortgage ate up the equity, and the debt made it possible for the bank to foreclose on the home if the parents could not make their payments.

Recently, I heard a doctor mention that she had $260,000 in student loans. She and her husband were making a good salary after graduating and realized that when they were paying their student loan back, they were actually paying less toward the loan principal because the interest rate had increased significantly. Let's say they were paying $20,000 a year, but the interest was $22,000 a year. Even though they were making their payments, they were still losing ground in the amount of $2,000 a year because of the interest rate balance and the deferments they had. They realized that if they continued to pay as they were, they were going to continue to lose ground, unless they increased the payments (which is what they ultimately did). Many people are still paying student loans well into their forties and fifties, making this a crisis for many Americans.

No Way Out

One of the things consumers reading this book should know is that government student loans are the only debt that cannot be discharged through bankruptcy. There are ways the government will get their money, such as garnishing your income tax refund or salary through your workplace. If you borrow money from the federal government for student loans, you will pay it back, one way or another. Some people think, "I will just go bankrupt." You can't go bankrupt on the government.

Today the average student-loan borrower takes more than ten years to repay a loan. Typically, a mortgage is financed for 30 years, although it is possible to obtain one for 10, 15, or 20 years. Any mortgage is usually financing an appreciating asset. If you are paying on it, and the asset is increasing in value, that is a positive thing. Student loans don't appreciate. It is all debt, and it's all a liability. Cars today have repayment terms of six or seven years, but typically most things don't take ten years to pay off except home mortgages. However, the average student loan repayment takes more than ten years. Half of the students pay off their federal student loans 20 years after they begin college. They graduated when they were 21 or 22 and then they are 42 and are just paying off their student loans.

In many cases, students may have to work 12 to 14 years before they even come close to achieving their financial goals even though they are making the salary they want to make based on their experience and education. Thus, people continually defer their payments because the lenders allow them to defer. When they defer, that doesn't mean the debt has gone away or that interest isn't still accruing. If they owed $50,000 at 4% ten years ago and then have ten years of deferments so they now owe $60,747. They still have the principal of $50,000 plus interest of $10,747. If they need more time to repay, the lenders are happy to give it to them, which allows them to make more money from the borrower.

Remember, the government is not going to let you walk away from this debt. You may have gotten married and have kids, and you're trying to save for their education. Those are some of the challenges we face with student loans. Also remember that half of the people who borrow require 20 years to pay it back.

What About Those Who Don't Graduate?

Degree completion is also a major factor related to student loan defaults. We don't talk about the individuals who often start school and drop out in their sophomore year after borrowing $15,000 to $20,000. They're challenged to pay because they don't have a degree, they still owe the money, but may not have the job they want or they are not making what they expected to make.

Imagine the challenges for those who didn't graduate and have to pay back $15,000 for something they never benefitted from because they didn't finish school. It would be like buying a car but never being able to drive it. When anyone accepts student loan debt and adds it on top of their mortgage payment, car payment, food, utilities and travel expenses, you can see how not having a budget or not managing their money can put someone in a difficult situation.

You have to understand that if you don't pay back a student loan, you're going to continually have problems with your debt structure. Students who graduated with excessive debt are about 10% more likely to say that it caused delays with major life events such as buying a home, getting married, or having children. They are also about 20% more likely to say their debt influenced their employment plans, causing them to take a job outside of their field to work more often than they desired, or to work more than one job.

What's more, the problem of students borrowing money and dropping out of school before they finish is getting worse. According to www.collegeatlas.org, here are the latest statistics for college dropout rates:

- 56% of college students who start a four-year college drop out by year six of their college career.
- Full-time students are 55% less likely to drop out of college than students who go to school exclusively part-time.
- Students who start college before turning 20 have a 13-22% lower chance of dropping out than those who start college after turning 20
- 70% of Americans will study at a four-year college, but less than two-thirds will graduate with a degree.
- 30% of college freshmen drop out after their first year of college.
- On average, a college dropout earns 35% or $21,000 less each year than a college graduate.
- Being unable to balance school, jobs, and family is cited as one of the top reasons for dropping out of college

While college is not for everyone, here are some other interesting facts about those who do not finish college from the same source (www.collegeatlas.org):

- Those without a degree are two times more likely to be unemployed than those with a college degree.
- Children from low-income households were 7.6 times less likely to complete a bachelor's degree.
- A male with a college degree earns approximately $900,000 more in gross media lifetime earnings than a male high school graduate.
- A female with a college degree earns $630,000 more in gross median lifetime earnings than a female high school graduate.
- According to a six-year study, about 20% more men drop out of college than women.
- A college degree has a higher return on investment for a graduate in the U.S. than in any other nation.
- More than 75% of students who are required to take remedial college classes never graduate.

A lot of people use their student loan money for Christmas shopping or other expenses, which they are not supposed to do. It seems like free money until they are 32 years old, owe $80,000, and realize they spent $10,000 of that money on frivolous things.

A Better Way

I didn't start my education in earnest until I was out of active-duty military. I took a few classes before then, but I did not excel initially. I went to school and never stayed one day on a college campus living in a dormitory. I don't know what it's like to live in a dorm because all my schooling was at night or on the weekends.

I have five earned degrees: an associate's degree, bachelor's degree, master's degree, another master's degree, and a doctorate. The associate's degree is in business with an emphasis on finances, insurance, and real estate; I have a bachelor's degree in business communication; a master's degree in public policy from Carnegie Mellon University; an MBA from Point Park University; and a doctorate in information systems and communication from Robin Morris University. I am an advocate for community college. I went to a Community College half time for four years to earn a two-year degree and I used my GI Bill. Community college is less expensive and class sizes are smaller. I then went to Carlow College, which accepted all of my courses from the Community College of Allegheny County. The class size was perfect, cost was low, and the quality of education and support was extremely high.

I completed graduate school at Carnegie Mellon University and paid it off quickly because I didn't want to have additional debt. Every time I graduated, I figured it would be the last time I went to school. Then I got the job with Fannie Mae, which had a great tuition reimbursement program. I was able to go and secure my MBA and my company paid for it all. When people are looking for a job, they should also look for what companies will give tuition assistance. Fannie Mae not only paid for my MBA in total but also 50% of my doctorate degree tuition.

Fannie Mae paid half of the more than $60,000 expense. That's how I financed my doctorate degree. To earn five degrees, it cost me approximately $167,000. Some of it was borrowed student loan money, some from employee reimbursements, and some was my own money. I certainly wasn't borrowing everything through student loans. You may not earn five degrees, but I had an employer who was willing to help out, and that made a big difference. Had I not had an employer helping me finance part of my education, I probably would not have been able to pay for a second master's degree and a doctorate.

There are several programs that people can put money in while their children are young and they are then guaranteed the money will be available later for their child's education. One is called a 529s and is a good plan because you can start saving at an early age for your child's higher education. Essentially, 529s are college savings plans that are exempt from federal taxes. You have to use the money for them to go to college and the question at an early age is: Will your child want to go to college? If you think they will, then a 529 plan is one of several good options to consider.

I urge you to research options and scholarships. Most in-state universities offer reduced tuition to individuals who live in that state. For example, residents can go to college for four years in Georgia for free if they have lived there long enough. Today there are many different ways to get assistance with education and it's worth it, even if in some cases the school is not someone's top choice.

People who work at colleges and universities can get tuition reimbursements. Employers who have tuition reimbursement plans will often pay for tuition if the degree is in the employee's field of work (they generally won't pay for an accounting degree if you are a nurse). Sometimes the employees must agree to stay at the company for a certain amount of time after they finish their degree.

Think Before You Borrow

The June 28, 2016 edition of *Consumer Reports* told the story of 1,500 Americans who were surveyed concerning the worth of student debt. They were asked if it translated into a better future and higher earnings return. The answers were eye-opening, and left many wondering why they borrowed as much as they did.

- 45% of people with student loan debt said that college was not worth the cost.
- 38% of those who said college wasn't worth the cost and didn't graduate.
- 69% have had trouble making loan payments.
- 78% earn less than $50,000 a year.
- 43% didn't get help from parents making financial aid decisions.
- 40% have had to cut back on day-to-day living expenses.
- 37% delayed savings for retirement or other financial goals.
- 28% delayed buying a house.
- 12% delayed marriage.
- 14% changed careers as a result of their student debt.

The report also stated, when asked if they would want to know how much a partner has in student debt before entering into a serious relationship, 44% said they would, while 36% said no. Forty-seven percent said that if they had to do it all over again, they would have accepted less financial aid. That means they would have gone to a less expensive school or tried to find another way to finance their college education.

I have spent more time on the issue of student loans because it is a hot topic that can often be thought of as something other than traditional debt. People are going to school and the assumption is that they will graduate, get good-paying jobs, and then make small payments to repay the loan and everything will work out. As I have explained, this is not always the case. The point is to approach a student loan with caution, understanding the ramifications of what you are about to do.

Let's move on in our financial literacy quest and talk a little about something called predatory lending, which can be a part of any of the debt we have already mentioned (except for student loans). Read on and perhaps you will read something new so you can be on the lookout for these practices in your own financial journey.

"If you're financially responsible,
your children have a much better chance
to grow up financially responsible.
No one has ever achieved financial fitness,
with a January resolution that's
abandoned by February."
- Suze Orman

Chapter 8
Don't Get Trapped in Predatory Lending

Predatory lending, which is prevalent in today's market, and it's nothing but a money grab by the predatory lenders. This type of lending is the unfair, deceptive, and duplicitous practice of imposing unfair or abusive loan terms and interest rates on borrowers. A good example of this would be the unfair practices that a national billion-dollar-bank practiced a few years ago. This multi-billion-dollar bank created millions of unauthorized checking and saving accounts for their customers. This was done so employees could earn bonuses for opening new accounts.

The bank ultimately agreed to spend $175 million to settle Federal accusations that it directed black and Latino borrowers into higher-cost loans and charged them excessive fees. Looking at the status of black women, a Home Mortgage Data Act study showed that middle- to upper-income African American women in 80% of the 100 cities surveyed were more likely to receive a high-cost subprime loan than other groups.

A former employee of the billion dollar national bank said that she and her co-workers purposely sold shoddy mortgages to would-be African

American homeowners, especially in certain markets like Prince George's County in Maryland. The first thing you should look out for is whether the lender is asking you for what seems to be higher than standard fees. This could be an indicator that they may be engaging in predatory lending.

There are what is called discount points with a loan, which are simply lenders' fees for making a loan. There is no standard list of fees or points; every lender has its own methodology for establishing points. In many cases, a predatory lender will tell someone their credit is so bad that they need to charge more fees to find a loan product for them. Most banks don't engage in predatory lending, but payday lenders often do. This is the reason credit is so important to consumers. When you have good credit, in some cases you pay less if you borrow.

The payday or predatory lenders often stipulate that you must pay a prepayment penalty. Why should you have to pay a fee to pay the money you borrowed back early? This is counterintuitive. If you owe money and have five years to pay it back, but choose to do so in three years, you should not be penalized with an early payback penalty.

Payday lenders are present, especially in low- and limited-income areas, and they will advance consumers money based on their upcoming paycheck because unfortunately, there are individuals who are predisposed to living paycheck-to-paycheck. When someone does not know how to manage their finances, they become susceptible to other sources to financing their addiction to debt, even when it means making poor choices such as borrowing from payday lenders. The payday lender will give them money when they need it and the borrower promises to pay it back when they next get paid. The problem is the money comes at a high cost, sometimes 20% of the loan amount. If they need $800 today, they may have to pay $960 back when they get paid.

If the borrower can't pay, the lender will simply charge more interest and extend the date for repayment to the next payday. The lender may say, "That's no problem. In fact, we'll lend you even more money and you can pay us in two weeks." Then in two weeks, the borrower will have to pay the $800 plus more fees. That may go on for a few more pay periods and before the borrower realizes it, they have paid $500 for the "privilege" of borrowing $800 of their own money over a period of a few months. There are also payday lenders online who are angling for businesses using the internet, and their ads are tempting: "Get $1,000 today with no need to pay it back for 90 days!" They are hoping borrowers will bite and then be hooked for a lot longer than 90 days.

The entire concept of predatory lending involves unfair practices.

Often, it's done in a way that people believe is the right way to do it. The lender may have a nice office or the borrower sees a person who looks professional. The lender seems intelligent and professional too, so it doesn't feel like a deal going the wrong way down a one-way street.

Years ago, people would seek loans on the street and we called it loan sharking. I am not saying predatory lending is the equivalent of that practice. If they explain things and the borrower signs the agreement, then it is legal. The concept is the same when consumers need quick money, are overextended, and have no savings. The lender offers a ready source of cash and the borrower will have to pay a high price to get it. It's appealing to the consumer and they often acquiesce to the circumstances for borrowing, even when it's a poor choice and clearly not in their favor.

Some people are so addicted to debt that they'll do whatever they need to do to buy whatever they want to buy. They will go to predatory lenders so they can get that quick fix by going out and spending more money. Then they do it all over again next month at some point, and they become addicted to debt. This is the reason predatory lenders find a ready-and-willing customer base: People are overextended, have no savings, and are often financially uneducated.

Speaking of savings, it's time to look at this important but often neglected practice in American households. Let's do that in the next chapter.

"I came out of my professional athletic career with a 450 credit score, no money in the bank to show for it, but I had an Ivy League degree. So I put that Dartmouth degree to good use and got a job on Wall Street. I hated it, but used the time to make connections and become financially literate."
- Brian Joseph White

Chapter 9

Don't Ask, Just Save

People in America don't save as much as they should, no matter what their income level is. A recent study showed that only 39% of Americans have enough savings to cover a $1,000 emergency. In other words, 61% of Americans could not come up with $1,000 if they needed to do so, and that amounts to millions of individuals. According to Bankrate's latest financial security index survey (www.bankrate.com), 34% of American households experienced a major unexpected expense over the past year. Here is how they would cover that $1,000 emergency expense:

- 39% said they could pay for the $1,000 emergency from their savings.
- 90% indicated they'd have to finance it with a credit card, and pay it off over time.
- 13% said they would have to reduce their spending on other things to cover it.
- 12% indicated they would have to borrow from family and friends to cover it.
- 5% said they would have to take out a personal loan to cover it.

When you study these percentages, using a credit card was the second most popular answer with 90% of respondents saying they would deal with the $1,000 emergency using plastic. Therein lies the challenge and problem because we're only talking about a $1,000 emergency, which can happen quickly. Car repairs, a new refrigerator, a leaky roof, or the deductible on health insurance are a few examples of an emergency that can occur in a moment's notice. Think about it: Nearly two-thirds of Americans could not come up with the needed cash. Could you handle a $1,000 emergency without borrowing?

A Gobanking rates survey from 2016 found that 69% of Americans have less than $1,000 in available savings (not retirement funds) and 34% had no savings at all. What's more, the median and average savings account balance in the U. S. is $5,200. The mean balance is $33,766.49, but households with higher incomes skew the numbers when the mean is calculated. Here are the average savings amounts by age.

- Under 35 years old—$1,580
- 35 to 44—$5,000
- 45 to 54—$6,500
- 65 to 74 it was $10,000
- 75 and over—$11,000

No matter what category you are in, these are extremely low amounts. If the money isn't available when the crisis strikes, then funds will need to be borrowed. It is no surprise that Americans with higher incomes have the disposable income to save more money, but it doesn't mean they do. Those who make less than $25,000 a year, according to the study, have only $500 in savings, while those making more than $116,000 a year have a mean of $50,000 in savings:

Savings by income:

- Under $25,000— $500
- $25,000 and $44,999— $1,500
- $45,000 to $69,999— $2,200
- $70,000 to $114,999— $5,400
- $116,000 and up— $115,000

Low-income earners are the least likely to have a savings account, but everyone should have one no matter what their level of income is. It doesn't matter if you save $30 or $500 a month, everyone should get into the habit of savings and start doing it early in life. The more you save, the more you will have for emergencies and you will become accustomed to the practice of putting money away.

Starting Early

Early in our marriage, my wife and I wanted to see what we were spending. We logged everything we spent money on for a full month. I didn't know what she spent during the day and she didn't know what I spent, so we tracked it for 30 days. She would buy coffee and some mints every day. I would buy a Snickers bar and a Pepsi, things like that. We didn't realize the things we were consistently and regularly spending money on amounted to enough to at least cover a monthly utility payment.

When we were done with this analysis, we realized we were spending somewhere around $120 a month on frivolous things like chewing gum, candy bars, soft drinks, and coffee, and that was before grande, venti, or trenta became household sizes for a cup of coffee. It made me wonder how much money people are spending when they don't measure or keep track of what they spend daily. We decided to take that money we were spending on frivolous things that we didn't need and save that amount. What if you did the same, how much would you save based on what you are spending, which will be different for everyone?

This is the kind of thing one needs to do in order to have some additional money for spending. You must also consider if you are a woman, then you earn on average $0.78 compared to the $1.00 that a male earns. Therefore, women must focus on saving money just to keep pace because men still on average out-earn women. The median savings account for males is about $7,000, while for females it is about $2,000.

The pay gap still exists among different races too. In America, white Americans earn more than their black or Hispanic counterparts. As you would expect, wealth and savings follow suit:

- White savings amount: $7,140
- Hispanic: $1,500
- Blacks: $1,000

The Lord Expects Increase

The Lord said it is permissible to earn interest. In fact, He expects us to do so. That's expected as a good steward. Let's look at a parable in the Bible, Matthew 25:30, that speaks about talents (which was a form of money at the time Jesus told this parable):

> [14]For the kingdom of heaven is as a man travelling into a far country, who called his own servants, and delivered unto them his goods.
>
> [15]And unto one he gave five talents, to another two, and to

another one; to every man according to his several ability; and straightway took his journey.

[16]Then he that had received the five talents went and traded with the same, and made them other five talents.

[17]And likewise he that had received two, he also gained other two.

[18]But he that had received one went and digged in the earth, and hid his lord's money.

[19]After a long time the lord of those servants cometh, and reckoneth with them.

[20]And so he that had received five talents came and brought other five talents, saying, Lord, thou deliveredst unto me five talents: behold, I have gained beside them five talents more.

[21]His lord said unto him, Well done, thou good and faithful servant: thou hast been faithful over a few things, I will make thee ruler over many things: enter thou into the joy of thy lord.

[22]He also that had received two talents came and said, Lord, thou deliveredst unto me two talents: behold, I have gained two other talents beside them.

[23]His lord said unto him, Well done, good and faithful servant; thou hast been faithful over a few things, I will make thee ruler over many things: enter thou into the joy of thy lord.

[24]Then he which had received the one talent came and said, Lord, I knew thee that thou art an hard man, reaping where thou hast not sown, and gathering where thou hast not strawed:

[25]And I was afraid, and went and hid thy talent in the earth: lo, there thou hast that is thine.

[26]His lord answered and said unto him, Thou wicked and slothful servant, thou knewest that I reap where I sowed not, and gather where I have not strawed:

[27]Thou oughtest therefore to have put my money to the exchangers, and then at my coming I should have received mine own with usury.

[28]Take therefore the talent from him, and give it unto him which hath ten talents.

[29]For unto every one that hath shall be given, and he shall have abundance: but from him that hath not shall be taken away even that which he hath.

³⁰And cast ye the unprofitable servant into outer darkness: there shall be weeping and gnashing of teeth.

God has given us the ability to make our own decisions and use our talents for good. We should be extremely dutiful as to how we handle His money, it is not our money; we are simply stewards of what He has given us. Always remember, God owns everything, we own nothing, but how we handle what He has given us matters. We should be wise with our finances; if not, why would we expect God to bless us financially if we don't handle wisely what He has already done for us?

Making poor choices, buying what we want without planning or regard for tomorrow, and being wasteful and unaccountable can all be detrimental to us and our families. Don't fall prey to the mismanagement of God's blessing on your life. God is the one who holds the jobs, health, financial increase, spouse, children, homes, cars, education and every good thing. You won't go wrong following His plan.

When reflecting on the passage of Scripture from Matthew 25:14-29, you may ask why the talent would be taken away from the person who had the least and given to the person who had the most. It's because the one who had the most talents demonstrated he knew what to do with what God had given him. Therefore, God took from the unproductive and gave to the productive. That sounds like a solid investment of resources to me. You can help the ministry, the widows, or the poor. If you take the talent and do nothing with it, don't expect God to give you more so you can do nothing with it. He gave it to you to do something, and that is to bring increase. How would you respond if God asked you what did you do with the talent He gave you? Think about that: Everyone who has, more will be given. We need to be able to take care of the widows and orphans and God's ministries. Use what God has given you to give more.

The parable of the rich man found in Luke 12:13-21 is worth mentioning here as well:

> ¹³ And one of the company said unto him, Master, speak to my brother, that he divide the inheritance with me.
>
> ¹⁴ And he said unto him, Man, who made me a judge or a divider over you?
>
> ¹⁵ And he said unto them, Take heed, and beware of covetousness: for a man's life consisteth not in the abundance of the things which he possesseth.
>
> ¹⁶ And he spake a parable unto them, saying, The ground of a certain rich man brought forth plentifully:

[17] And he thought within himself, saying, What shall I do, because I have no room where to bestow my fruits?

[18] And he said, This will I do: I will pull down my barns, and build greater; and there will I bestow all my fruits and my goods.

[19] And I will say to my soul, Soul, thou hast much goods laid up for many years; take thine ease, eat, drink, and be merry.

[20] But God said unto him, Thou fool, this night thy soul shall be required of thee: then whose shall those things be, which thou hast provided?

[21] So is he that layeth up treasure for himself, and is not rich toward God.

Our intellectual capacity is often a key to how we will handle the issue of spending and being susceptible to advertising. I mentioned earlier that you may not really believe you will ever be able to live without debt. If that's what you believe, then that is what is destined to happen.

It's important to keep your mind focused on the Lord and your goals. The Word says if you keep your mind stayed on him, he will keep you in perfect peace. And in order to be successful as it relates to all things, including income and debt, you have to keep your mind on Him. It will keep you laser focused on the goal of staying out of debt.

Developing the habit of saving money will help you stave off the need to utilize debt when an emergency hits you or even when you are looking to make a legitimate, necessary purchase like a home. Saving money necessitates you foregoing something now, which is called delayed gratification, so you can prepare and manage your resources for future purchases. It's imperative that when you do begin to save, you don't stop there, but you also invest so you can earn interest on what you've saved. I urge you to take this chapter seriously and do what you can, regardless of where you are in your financial journey, to begin saving money.

I trust you've grasped the theme of my book by now: Don't get addicted to debt but if you are, you can disavow this horrible state of affairs. We covered topics such as savings, credit cards, home mortgages, student loans, car purchases, and predatory lending. What changes have you decided to make as a result of what you have read?

It's time to move on to the next section where I will address the topics of budgeting, gambling (no short-cuts to financial success), generosity, and other concepts important for you to know as you grow in your financial awareness. After section two, I'll have some concluding thoughts to share with you.

Section Two
Practical Steps

"I realize what it means to be
financially comfortable and I want to be that.
But I'm lucky enough to be in that position.
And I'm also careful, I save 38% of my earnings after
expenses, before taxes."
- David Duval

Chapter 10
Debt Addiction Intensified

Each year, corporations spend large amounts of money to personalize their marketing messages and discover new tactics to encourage consumers to buy their products. There is one group particularly vulnerable to such efforts and they are compulsive buyers. These are folks who buy because it meets a need or helps cover another need, providing temporary relief, until the bills come due. Buying has never been easier with the internet, Amazon, eBay, PayPal, Wal-Mart, and online buying clubs that accept credit cards for all kinds of services and products, making shopping easy and a 24/7 practice. Can't sleep? You can surf the web and find that new sweater you want, on sale with free shipping no less.

This is another form of the addiction, and money spent must be repaid at some point. When it's not, it can have serious implications for individuals, families, and society as a whole. Advertising drives and fuels the need to buy, have more, and spend more money the consumer rarely has.

Not all advertising is bad or negative. Advertising educates and informs consumers as to what is available along with the features and benefits.

The ultimate goal of advertisers, manufacturers, and retailers, however, is to get consumers to part with their hard-earned cash, at any cost.

As I write this book, there are many ad campaigns that saturate the airwaves, as usual. Who hasn't seen an insurance ad on television? Some of them are simply positioning the company's brand in your mind so when you need insurance, you will think of them, maybe singing their jingle or laughing at the image of their spokesperson in your mind. They pull you in so easily. One credit card advertisement I saw suggested to use their card to pay off existing debt. That doesn't get you out of debt, but people fall for this all the time. The interest rate may be zero for 90 days, but the due date is looming. Do not fall for this, or do not fall for this again!

Compulsive buyers are more vulnerable to advertising than non-compulsive buyers, which is the reason why there are more people in debt today than ever before. If we can pay our bills, we may not see ourselves as a compulsive shopper, but that doesn't mean we aren't. Consumers can get used to spending to their maximum capability, which is when trouble knocks on the door. You suddenly have a major debt on your hands with no way out. Consumers suffer because they seldom face their addiction and are going through withdrawal.

Unfortunately, that's what advertisers want. They want you to be addicted and feel compelled to use your credit card, which can lead to compulsiveness. They want you to come out every weekend or to swipe your card to pay for fast food or for the ever-present sales, which aren't really sales, just prices inflated and then marked down so they appear as a sale.

At the same time, consumers must be cognizant of what they are signing whenever they are asked to make that kind of commitment. We know the question, "Did you read the fine print?" Most people still don't read it, proceed, and sign without an understanding, and suffer the consequences. In some cases, they were too embarrassed to say they didn't understand. Don't be embarrassed, because it's better to get a full understanding up front as opposed to getting a full understanding in retrospect.

When you sign those documents, it's hard to get out of them, even if you didn't know what you were signing. Don't be too quick to sign because somebody is offering you money. Don't cash the check in the mail that instructs you to sign and you get $5,000. If you don't understand the ramifications of doing so, you can't blame the lender. Much of the responsibility for that is on the consumer. Don't be so addicted to debt that you are not willing to do the homework necessary to reduce or eliminate your debt risk.

Your financial decisions have consequences, either good or bad, and have generational implications. Children often follow what their parents do and that sometimes includes amassing a large debt load. You can make a difference by making sure that doesn't happen. You may need to borrow in some cases, but not to your detriment or that of your family. If you are addicted to debt, there is still time to turn things around and get out and stay out.

Predictive Technology

You need to be familiar with a new term relating to technology that will have a significant impact on how advertisers look at and determine how they market to consumers. That phrase is *predictive technology*. My hypothesis is that predictive technology will allow marketers to determine, based on data extrapolated from past purchases, bank loans, mortgages, and credit scores, whether or not you will be a spender or a saver; whether or not you will ultimately go into more debt than you can handle or if you will be debt-averse; or if you will be able to manage the debt. Based on the predictive clues in the data, marketers and advertisers will be able to determine how they advertise and market to you.

This predictive technology is not being gathered for the purpose or marketing at present. It is my opinion, however, that at some point, it will be used for this purpose. It's important from a generational perspective to manage money well because the impact of what you do today can have an impact on those who come after you: your kids, grandkids, and so forth.

What predictive technology will be able to do, in my opinion, is determine if someone is a poor credit risk and conclude that a company should not market to that person. It may predict you will ultimately go into bankruptcy or encounter financial problems, and therefore the advertisers won't market to you, companies won't hire you, and insurance companies will not insure you. You won't get the benefit of having the products and services others may be privy to, solely based on predictive technology. Of course, this scenario is hypothetical at present.

All consumers should have the ability to purchase and make financial decisions, just like anyone else. The question is: How do you do that if you don't have an opportunity to even know what products and offers to accept? That could put you and people like you in a difficult predicament. It is important that you be responsible because the technology being developed today will have a significant impact on your life going forward.

Hypothetically, when you walk into a bank to borrow, even though you may have good credit at the time you walk in, the lender could say they are not going to loan to you based on predictive technology. Based on their technology, they've already concluded there is a good chance you will ultimately fail in your efforts to repay them. They predict you are going to go into so much debt, or there is a likelihood that you will simply not succeed in life. Therefore, even though you may be fine from a credit-risk perspective at the time, they are not going to loan you money. For now it's not how things are done, but it is possible.

Is that possible and plausible? Absolutely! It's just another reason why you must make sure you don't get addicted and become a poor manager of your finances, it will have long-term consequences. Make sure you don't bite off more than you can handle. Keep in mind, technology will matter, and you will not be able to manipulate the data. The only thing you can do is manage your finances well, so the use of whatever technologies are developed will not have a negative impact on you.

When I was a lender and bank manager in the '80s, we made loan decisions based on pulling a credit report and looking at the three Cs: credit, collateral, and capacity to pay. We knew who came into the bank from our communities and we made credit decisions based on our ability to assess their credit, their accounts, and who they were (reputation). There were no credit scores back then.

Move forward twenty years to the advent of credit scoring. It's not so far-fetched to think that predictive technology will be used to do the same thing that occurred when credit scoring arrived on the scene. Keep in mind, credit scoring was not around in the '80s and currently neither is predictive technology for consumers, but certainly it has a high probability of being developed and used I believe.

Addiction Defined

In case you still don't believe you may be addicted, read the definition of addiction closely.

> An addiction is to have a medically or *psychologically* significant addiction; to occupy oneself or involve oneself in something habitually; to cause to use something on a regular or dependent basis; devoted to a particular activity or thing; a strong and harmful need to regularly have something or do something; great interest in something or a need *to do or have something*.

When you look at this definition, it's obvious being addicted to debt is highly plausible.

People who are addicted to debt are no different in terms of the effects than people who are addicted to drugs, food, or any other substance. I want you to read this book and find a way out. If you're not in it, don't get in it, because this is one of the most devastating problems we have in

America today. It's a silent killer too. People who are addicted to alcohol have Alcoholics Anonymous to help them through their difficulty. If addicted to drugs, there's Narcotics Anonymous. When you're addicted to debt, there aren't a lot of places to go and get help, which is one reason why I wrote this book. You have to search for it and really want to be set free. You have to be willing to change your lifestyle and adopt a new value system. I know of no addicted-to-debt programs where people meet weekly and affirm their problem. There are financial literacy and education programs, but they don't typically deal with debt addiction. No one can be there every time you pull out the plastic or borrow more money. That's why I'm raising this awareness to as many as I can now.

Many people don't consider that going to the mall six or seven times a month to shop can be an addiction, or eating at restaurants six times a month, or spending $9.00 a day on coffee and a breakfast sandwiches can all be expressions of an addiction. Spending $280 a month without equivocation, experiencing frequently past-due utility bills, or not having the money to pay a light or water bill are the signs. There is a difference between being broke and being addicted. All too often we lay claim to not having enough money, when in reality, that is not the issue; it's the addiction to debt that's at issue. Someone addicted to debt rarely can be made whole; the addiction will take every cent that person has, and will put them in a deficit position if they are not careful.

Companies know this game too. They want you to pay the least amount on the credit card balances because when you pay $20 a month on a $2,000 balance, it will take you years to pay it off. Their goal for you is *not* for you to pay it off. There are debt consolidation services that will help people pay off their credit card debt, but only if the consumer is disciplined enough to stop using cards. Many companies and individuals don't know how to do debt consolidation, so I don't always agree that it's the best strategy. If they take all their debt and have one payment, pay it off, and clean up their credit, they start receiving new credit cards because their credit load is reduced.

Or people put all their debt on their house as a second mortgage. Then it's going to be for another five or ten years before it's paid off. If they start using credit cards and buy a car, they have all the debt they previously had on the house payment while increasing their debt again. That's why consolidation may not be the best answer. It is an answer, but it may not be the best, depending on the person. If you're addicted to debt, it's not good. The likelihood that you will repeat bad habits and end up in more debt is highly possible.

One of the practices you can embrace, and I have referred to it throughout the book, is developing and following a reasonable budget plan. Some people react to the concept because it requires discipline and restricts their financial freedom, which is exactly what it is supposed to do. I have referred to budgeting long enough; let's examine it more closely in the next chapter, Don't *think* you know, *know* you know about budgeting successfully.

Chapter 11
Budgeting

Budgeting is a daunting concept to some individuals, although it shouldn't be. Often individuals feel it's difficult to stick to a budget for fear it can become unrealistic or a reminder of what a person is constantly not doing right. In reality, a budget is nothing more than a road map helping you get to a financial place in life. Think of it as a GPS guide when you want to drive somewhere that you haven't been and don't know how to get there. You put in the coordinates or address, zip code, or city and then the GPS calculates the route from your present location, along with what time you will arrive.

There are times when the GPS notifies you to go a different route due to a traffic jam or roadwork ahead. In life, there may be times when you deviate from your budget, but it's important that you stick with the plan and get back on track. It's not getting off track that is the problem, but rather staying off track that will get you where you do not want to go. If you put in the correct coordinates and stick to it, the budget, like the GPS, will guide you there. Instead of the word *budget*, think of how you are going to get there financially. To do so will require strict adherence to the map laid out with the path to follow. If you can do this and stay focused, you eventually will get on the path to debt-free living.

One way to get off track on your budget is to go over your credit limit on credit cards. This happens when your credit limit is $1,000, but you spend $1,200. You're going to pay a fee for going over your limit. Don't make ill-advised purchases for things that don't benefit you. That's what you have to think about when you are shopping. What is it that you need, not what you want? Also, don't go grocery shopping while you are hungry, or you will exceed your budget. Ask yourself: Am I making an impulse purchase or purchasing something I need or of value? Do you have to buy the most expensive bottle of perfume or cologne? Of course, the answer is "No."

Have a Plan

To get answers to those questions, you must look at your budget. It is a good thing to review your budget on a weekly basis because until you know your budget like you know your income, you are not going to identify the problem when you are in the store or browsing online on Cyber Monday. When you are in a store, you should know that you are not going to be able to get your car fixed or pay the winter electric bill if you go over your budget. Your budget dictates everything financial and you should put money aside because eventually something will go wrong with the car, or your home will need repairs, or a faucet will leak.

Something will happen, so you need to prepare for it. These inevitable expenses must be reflected in your budget, if it's to be realistic. One of the mistakes individuals make when establishing a budget is they force balance, a term I learned when I was a bank teller. When you force balance, you essentially figure out a way to make it balance by changing the numbers, even though it's not a true reflection of what's really occurring.

You must have a plan, just like a game plan in sports. When athletes go out on the field or court or when companies develop a business, there is a plan. In sports, there is a game plan every week or every few days because they are playing a different team, regardless of the sport. Each team has a plan of attack, and you need your own plan of attack. Think of it as an attack, because this cannot be a passive undertaking if you are going to achieve your financial goals.

If you're going to the mall and the game plan is to spend $120 there because that is all you have in discretionary income, that must be at the forefront of your mind. You don't overcome your addiction and get out of debt with a disorganized approach. It is a process, and if you don't have a budget, which is your game plan, the likelihood of getting out and staying out is nil. Have you been to a jewelry store lately? The jewelry is under lights that make it look like it is the most beautiful jewelry in the world simply to appeal to your senses. If you take the jewelry out of the light, you will then see what it really looks like. Consumers can get mesmorized by the lights, which are there to entice you to purchase. Even the mannequins make you want to purchase; they almost look real. The mannequins come in all sizes and shapes to make you feel what they have on is a perfect fit for you. The stores will do everything and anything to get your dollar!

As long as consumers spend, advertisers will use deceptive ads, gimmicks, testimonials, celebrities, musicians, and anyone else to bank your dollar into their profitability. That's why more people are broke today than ever before. People are bombarded with ads, and then they think, *I have to have this product to make my teeth whiter. Then I will feel better about myself.* That may be the case, but it's going to cause you to spend over your budget and feel justified in doing so. Don't do it, because if you do, you will continue doing this and rarely can someone with this tendency ever become debt free.

Don't forget about savings in your budget. If you want products you need, you have to learn to say no to the ones you don't need. When you purchase items using cash, you are much more judicious in your purchasing choices. This is because with cash, the money is gone immediately and you feel the loss. With credit, it seems like you have not lost a lot and only have to pay a few dollars a month for the payment. It's a much better feeling to know you have no Christmas bills coming due in January. Once you begin to shy away from credit and embrace a credit-less lifestyle, you will reap the benefits of increased cash, and more deliberate purchases that have meaning.

Except when purchasing a home, use cash to purchase everything else if possible. It will take some time to get to an all-cash way of doing business, but as you now know, it's possible. I wanted to share my credit report on the next page as of March 4, 2019. It took some years to function in a debt- driven society where no debt is considered abnormal and maxed out credit cards and payday lenders seem normal. Having been debt free for more than fourteen years is a blessing and an exhilarating and unbelievable feeling, so much so, that once my wife and I achieved this goal, we have a strong aversion to signing a car note or any other debt instruments.

Debt is a bad word to us, and this is achievable for anyone at any income level. Credit is very important, however, today insurance companies pull your credit report and employers do too. Medical professionals want to know if you're a great, good, or poor credit risk, so it's necessary to have a good credit or FICO score.

Latest Credit Score

As of 03/04/2019

809

EXCELLENT

Howard Slaughter

Latest Credit Summary

Your Credit Summary highlights the information in your credit file that is most important in determining your credit standing by distilling key credit information into one easy-to-read summary.

CREDIT REPORT as of 03/04/2019

Open Accounts	Total#	Balance	Available ⁇	Credit Limit ⁇	Debt to Credit	Monthly Payment Amount ⁇	Accounts with a Balance
Mortgage	0	$0	N/A	N/A	N/A	$0	0
Installment	0	$0	N/A	N/A	N/A	$0	0
Revolving	3	$0	$0	$0	0%	$0	0
Other	0	$0	N/A	N/A	N/A	$0	0
Total	3	$0	$0	$0	0%	$0	0

No open balances reported.

Equifax Complete™ Premier Plan

You don't need a college degree to make and keep a budget, and if you have a degree, don't think one isn't important for you. A budget is important for everyone. Sit down, plan your expenses, compare them to your income to make sure they truly balance. Be honest. Make sure your budget includes money for savings and the unexpected, and then stick to it. If you have to deviate, do what you can to get back on track as soon as possible. A budget is a work of art that always requires adaptations to make it more accurate.

Let's move on now to look at an issue I see as a growing problem among both the poor *and* the wealthy, and even some Christians, and that is the proliferation of legalized gambling.

Chapter 12
What About Gambling?

Many people believe that gambling is a better option to gain wealth than having to develop budgets or invest money in the stock market, mutual funds, money market account, or in a savings account. No matter how anyone looks at it, the idea that risking your money on a chance to win at gambling is not how you cover debt. All too often, Americans gamble, hoping to win money but in most cases, they lose money. The statistics verify this point clearly.

For example, you have a one-in-175,000,000 chance to win the lottery if you play. Think of it this way. There are just over 350,000,000 people in the United States, so you have the chance to win the lottery, two out of 350,000,000 chances each time you play. With these odds, it is inconceivable that someone would continue to play against the odds, but people do it all the time, enriching state and government treasuries. Actually, you really are the loser even if you win, the government is the real lottery winner no matter how often you play.

The idea that the lottery benefits senior citizens, something States have claimed when seeking voter permission to establish legalized gambling, is undeterminable. If you want to take a chance playing the lottery or for entertainment, go ahead. When you consider the amount of money you regularly spend playing the lottery or gambling at casinos or online, you will see that you have lost more money than you have made.

Even in many cases for those who have won a big lottery payout, those individuals often don't retain their winnings. The likelihood is that in five years, many who have won the lottery have gone broke even after winning millions of dollars. In a sense, if you win, you still lose because you are most likely going to end up broke or even bankrupt. Does it truly benefit you to play the lottery from any angle you consider?

My wife and I went on a trip to Las Vegas years ago and we toured the Grand Canyon and Hoover Dam, which was a great place to visit. When we got off the plane, we heard a lot of bells dinging. Unbeknownst to us, there are slot machines and gambling in McCarran International Airport, even in the restrooms. We saw people get off the plane who didn't wait to get to the Strip to start gambling. Conversely, there were people going home who were gambling right up until they had to board their plane.

We stayed on the Vegas Strip and after dinner one evening, we went shopping and sightseeing. At about 12:30 AM, we decided to call it an evening. As we were walking through the casino to get to the elevators to our room, we saw a senior citizen who appeared to be in her eighties playing the slots. The next morning when we went to breakfast, we walked the same way and guess who we saw? You got it; we saw the same senior citizen. Apparently, she had played all night long. I don't know if she won or not, but she was still playing. The likelihood of her having won, at least winning big, was slim. All night long she got enjoyment from being at the slot machine. That was not a beneficial or realistic way for her to increase her wealth or spend her money—and it isn't for you either.

Instead of playing the lottery, I urge you to look at other ways you can earn more money (see my earlier chapter on making money). If you follow the principles of God by giving your tithe and your offering, and focus on being a blessing to others by helping them, you will be fine. The Scriptures tell us not to take thought for tomorrow, for God holds tomorrow. As a Christian, we should continue to help others and by doing so, we can rest assured that God will take care of us. Taking a risk and wasting your money on gambling is not the best choice for your hard-earned money. The lottery is like a vacuum; it just cleans you out every time you use it.

There are some interesting statistics related to gambling trends. I recently discovered that as many as 750,000 young people between the ages of 14 and 21 have a gambling addiction. I hope you are not one of them. Statistics also show that people between the ages of 20 and 30 have the highest rate of gambling problems. As you can see, gambling addiction starts early in life for many individuals who are caught up in the gaming game. One statistic stated that a person is better off financially to pick up a single penny on the sidewalk and do nothing else with it for two years. This person would be better with one penny as opposed to trying to gamble it and make money. In other words, you would at least still have the penny if you didn't gamble!

In the article Gambling to pay off debt, it stated a person was going to take their bonus check from work to the casino because they'd have "better odds" of paying off more debt than if they would just apply it to the principle balance of their outstanding credit card. The person had about $20,000 in debt at 20% interest. The question she did not consider is what would happen if she lost at the craps table? She lost the bonus money in this scenario, so she didn't have enough money to pay off her debt and was far worse off than before. This seems to me to be an awkward strategy for getting out of debt, but as I mentioned earlier, debt causes people to make irrational decisions again and again!

You Can't Win

In an article in *Life Science* written by Michael Shacklefort, who is a math and gambling expert, he explained that the worst gambling game you can play is the lottery. The reason he gave is that the house edge is 50%. Once you understand how bad a bet on a lottery ticket is, according to Michael, you will probably never play again. What did he mean by the house has an edge of 50%? If you bet $10 on the lottery, you are mathematically expected to lose $5. No matter what you play or how much you play, the house is already ahead of the curve by 50%. In theory, the most you could win is 50% of what you bet. In this case, if you bet $10, you are expected to lose $5 and keep $5, not great odds or return. So if you gamble $1,000, you will perhaps get $500 back but you will have lost $500, and that amount (losses) keeps going up the more you gamble.

Our national addiction to debt causes us to look for easy money. Also, because we idolize those who have a lot of money, we want what they have. Some individuals inherited their money from someone else's hard work. Others earned it themselves through hard work or through having a business idea that paid great returns. Still others were in a career that paid handsomely, like entertainment or professional sports. My point is that there is a reason the individuals we idolize have money, but rarely was it gained by gambling.

How do you find a way to make more money without spending more money? How do you get ahead without getting behind? The reality is that it takes discipline, hard work, and the stick-to-it-iveness that allows one to gain in an appropriate way. Yes, a few do win the lottery. Some win at the casinos, but by-and-large, the majority of Americans don't win. Even when they do win, there are still consequences to that win. It is imperative you understand your chances of winning the lottery, which is lessened significantly when you are betting against the house and millions of others.

Only so many people can win the lottery. This is not to say that it is rigged or fixed, but a simple fact that only so many people will win. The more people play, the higher your chances are of not winning! A way to increase your wealth and stay out of debt is to be prudent, focused, and committed to a strategy that works instead of one you *hope* works. You won't meet many people (if any) whose story is that they became debt free or who learned how to manage their money because they won the lottery. Those testimonials are few and far between.

Don't gamble your money away. Focus on a sure thing, not on a hopeful outcome. Today more than ever before, people are looking for a way out. That isn't the way when you consider the negative implications of gambling and lottery winnings. If you took every dollar you spent on gambling and/or the lottery over the past five years, how much would you have saved? What would have happened if you had kept that money and invested it? What would your return be? It may seem like a small amount when you gamble or play the lottery for $3 or $4 a day, but it does add up.

It's your money, and you have worked hard for it. Don't give it away to someone who doesn't need it, meaning the government or a casino. If you want to give your money away, there are many places where it would be beneficial and they would put that money to use for good things. Playing the lottery and gambling are tantamount to throwing your money away, and none of us can afford to do that.

Gambling Statistics by Race

According to a Gallup poll in July 2016 reported by Joe Setyon, nearly two-thirds of Americans (64%) admit they have gambled over the last year. The poll also found that nearly half (49%) of those interviewed said they had bought a lottery ticket over the past twelve months; 26% visited a casino; 15% participated in an office pool; and 10% bet on a professional sporting event. Forty percent of those with annual incomes of $36,000 or lower said they had purchased a state lottery ticket within the past year as compared to 56% of those who made between $36,000 and $89,999 and

53% who made $90,000 or more. Moreover, 47% of those interviewed with a high school education or less bought a state lottery ticket within the last twelve months, compared to 53% of those with a technical or college degree and 45% of those with a post-graduate education.

The National Center for Responsible Gaming in a report acknowledged that gambling problems are common among all racial and ethnic groups in the United States. There is new evidence that African Americans are more likely to experience gambling-related problems than white Americans, but these differences in problem and pathological gambling (PPG) among people of different races are not well understood.

A recent study analyzed data from the National Epidemologic Survey on Alcohol and Related Conditions, the largest study on psychiatric disorders in the United States. They compared black and white respondents on measures of gambling behavior, mental health, PPG, and the co-occurrence of the mental health disorders, and gambling among a national representative sample of 32,316 black and white adults in the United States. Blacks responded at 96% and were more likely than white respondents (45%) to exhibit past year PPG.

In December 2018, I read a story about two nuns at a Catholic school in California accused of embezzling $500,000 in school funds to use on gambling and vacations. These nuns allegedly stole this money over a ten-year period of time from Saint James Catholic School in Torrance, California. This is the level of unimaginable behavior that comes with the addiction of gambling, which is often fueled by needing more money because of the debt load people carry. Even nuns are not immune to the imposing power of money if they have to steal money to fuel their addiction. Where are we going that we can't trust those who have taken an oath to care and be concerned for those who need help, but would rather steal money in order to take a chance on winning more money? Some want the vacations and other luxury items, but in many cases, they are looking to rid themselves of the debt they have been building up for years.

Gambling Defined

The definition of gambling will not surprise you. If you believe it is an opportunity and not chance, you should pay attention to this definition:

> To take risky action in the hope of a desired result or the activity
> or practice of playing at a game of chance for money or other
> stakes. Gambling is the wagering of money, or something of
> value, on an event with an uncertain outcome.

These definitions ought to scare you when it comes to gambling because they are overwhelming bad and not in your favor. Contrast that definition with the definition of *invest*, which is to

> Expend money with the expectation of achieving a profit or material result by putting it into financial schemes, shares, or property, or by using it to develop a commercial venture; provide or endow someone or something with a particular quality or attribute.

> Investing is the act of committing money or capital to an endeavor, business, project, real estate, etc., with the expectation of obtaining an additional income or profit. Investing can also include the amount of time you put into the study of a company in which you are considering an investment.

When you consider both definitions, which is really you?

I believe in generosity and giving to charitable causes, but I am opposed to giving with the intent to get something back. There is a great reward in giving, and God is watching and can bless the giver, but to count on it as a financial strategy hoping for a quick return is ill-advised and immature. Let's spend some time in the next chapter looking at the importance of a lifestyle of giving as an antidote to greed and consumerism, which causes some people to buy and accumulate more and more things.

Chapter 13
Give Your Way Out

There are exceptions due to unexpected loss of income, fraud, medical bills, or other unanticipated twists and turns of life. Most debt is likely because we focused on our wants and desires, instead of the needs of others or the ministry, thus neglecting to follow God's principles. You wanted a new car, so you bought one, but it came with a large monthly payment that exceeded your vehicle budget line item. You wanted new clothes, a vacation, or a boat, so you borrowed the money and purchased those things (which depreciate the minute you purchase them).

Oftentimes, people shop when they are depressed or had what they consider a bad day and they believe shopping can make them feel better. Nevertheless, if it causes you to exceed your budget, borrow more money, or even spend money you don't have, you are a person who is simply out of control with your finances.

I was contemplating titling this book *Give Your Way Out,* but I was concerned that some readers would misunderstand the concept or intent of the title. The premise of *Give Your Way Out* of debt is still applicable. It is based on giving your tithes and offerings as God's word commands you to do, which is still relevant and must be done. There is a danger, however, in thinking there is an easy way out of debt. At some point, you must address the attitude and thinking that got you into debt in the first place. Part of that attitude could have been selfishness, which is a problem common to us all. As children, we usually have to be taught to share; it does not come to us naturally.

Change Your Attitude

Therefore, when I say that giving must be an important aspect of dealing with debt, I am referring to a change of attitude and a different mindset when it comes to money. That attitude is best described by the words of Jesus found in Luke's gospel:

> "Judge not, and ye shall not be judged. Condemn not, and ye shall not be condemned: Forgive, and ye shall be forgiven. Give, and it shall be given unto you: good measure, pressed down, and shaken together, and running over shall men give into your bosom. For with the same measure that ye mete withal it shall be measured to you again" (Luke 6:37-38).

These two verses summarize the shift in principles the Lord requires if you are going to prosper, and be in health, not just in finances, but in your overall lifestyle. There are two words in these verses that stand out to me: _forgive_ and _give_. If it is mercy, then we give mercy. If forgiveness, then we forgive. If it is money, then we give money or other resources we may have in our possession, such as our talents in an area that can benefit others.

One of the problems with debt is that you can't be generous because your money is tied up, even though giving to others is an exhilarating feeling. If you see a need, you want to help, but can't and it causes you to look the other way because you have nothing to give. Of course, the answer is not to borrow money to give, but to make room in your budget, pay down, and then payoff your debt so you can be a giver, not a taker.

Think of it this way: If you were able to take all the money you pay in interest and give that money to your church, a family in need, or your favorite charity, how much would it be? What impact would that money have in the lives and ministries of others? It would no doubt be significant.

Giving is not a manipulative process, a short-cut, or a technique so you can get out of debt. You should determine after reading this book that you are going to be known as a giver _now_, not later, not when you hope you'll have more money, not when the circumstances are more favorable, not when you get that next pay raise, but right now. You can give your time, talents, and other resources, so it doesn't have to be monetary.

People often think they must give large sums of money to be considered generous. That is the wrong mentality. It is my belief that God requires us to tithe on our gross income, which is 10% of your income before taxes, 401K payments, health payments, or any other initiated deductions. If you make $5,000 gross income a week, that's $500 or 10% in tithes, if you earn $1,000, its $100, and so on. This concept seems so simple to figure out, but most churches don't have all or even most of those in attendance giving a full 10% gross of their income annually.

Statistically, only about three to five percent of churchgoers who give to their church do so through tithing. God does not require the person giving $100 to increase to match someone whose tithe is more, and He does not more highly favor the one who gives $500. Your blessing comes from obediently following the principle of giving what God requires. God honors obedience and a generous heart, as written in Luke's gospel:

> And He looked up and saw the rich men casting their gifts into the treasury. And He saw also a certain poor widow casting in thither two mites. And He said of a truth, "I say unto that this poor widow has cast in more than they all: for all these have of their abundance cast in unto the offering of God; but she of her penury hast cast in all the living that she had" (Luke 21:1-4).

Jesus noticed and honored the woman not because of how much she gave, but how much she had left *after* she gave, which was nothing. She had given all she had! God is not looking for large gifts from you; He is looking for liberality. If you have some time and you devote it to help another person when you could have helped yourself, God honors that. If you have a gift or talent and you make it available to help others, even when it is inconvenient or costs you something, God honors that too. These are the characteristics we must all exhibit when it comes to money and serving the Lord.

Reluctance to Give

Some people believe if they keep what they have, they can build wealth from that, but this is not biblical. Try doing it God's way; you can't lose if you do. When you become debt free, then you can cultivate a lifestyle of giving and generosity even more. I'd suggest to start cultivating that lifestyle *now*, giving what you have and learning to serve others are God-given and God-honoring attributes.

Some individuals are reluctant to give for many reasons, and I understand that, but if that is you, learn to think differently. Give of your talents and resources, and make a difference where you are with what you have *today*, tomorrow is not promised to any of us. I know from personal experience that when my wife and I decided we were going to be givers, as God's word said, it was at that point the blessings of God began to overtake us. Remember, God loves a cheerful giver.

A newly-married young man needed a car, but didn't have a lot of money to buy one. His father-in-law wanted to help and had a second car. He gave the married couple the car, but they had to make the remaining payments on the car. About a week later, he went to his son-in-law and said, "I was led to give you the car without any additional payments." The father-in-law was blessed because he followed the leading of the Lord and his son-in-law saw a tangible expression of what it means to give.

How do you think the family members felt because of this transaction? I'm sure they were all joyful, both the giver and the recipient. That is the behavior I am urging you to embrace because you will have experienced what debt free really means, not just taking care of yourself, but to position yourself to help others. You don't have to wait, you can start living that kind of life right now. This requires a lifestyle change and that's why many people won't ever get there. I want you to remember that you must change the way you think, which requires seeking out different philosophical methodologies that will lead you to new ways of thinking, like I pray this book will do.

It's important to understand the way to get and stay out of debt is to give your way out. Some individuals don't believe this concept, because they don't understand how they can gain something while simultaneously giving something. I admit, it may seem oxymoronic to believe this financial faith move works, but it is true and does work! If you don't have the faith to believe this when you give, you will receive, you are teetering on an imbalance in your financial future. Ultimately, people have made mistakes misusing the principle by giving so they can receive. It's important to exhibit more faith and trust in the Lord who will give us an abundance according to His word, which is pressed down, shaken together, and running over (see Luke 6:38).

The Benefits of Generosity

God's principle of return is not always based on monetization that results in financial remuneration. If you give money or something else of value in your possession, does that mean God will only give to you in accordance to what you have given? If you give, can you reap the benefits in other ways like health, relationships, or simply His favor and protection?

And what about the benefits you cannot see? Is there a chance you were overlooked in your company's latest layoff, not because you were the smartest, but because it was given back to you because you gave?

God has blessed my career, not just financially, but with the opportunity to do meaningful work. At one time, I was the Regional Director of Fannie Mae's Business Center in Southwestern Pennsylvania. The Federal National Mortgage Association (FNMA), better known as Fannie Mae, is a United States government-sponsored enterprise and, since 1968, a publicly-traded company. Founded in 1938, the corporation's purpose is to expand the secondary mortgage market by securitizing mortgages in the form of mortgage-backed securities, allowing lenders to reinvest their assets into more lending and in effect increasing the number of lenders in the mortgage market by reducing the reliance on locally-based savings and loan associations and thrifts. As of 2018, Fannie Mae is ranked #21 on the Forbes 500 ranking of the largest U.S. corporations by total revenue.

I didn't seek this job; it sought me. When I was first approached about Fannie Mae's interest in opening an office in Pittsburgh, I gave them a list of names for the job. I wasn't interested in the job and as a banker, I had never worked in anything but retail banking. After six months, they had not found anyone and I got a call from the officials saying that they were coming to Pittsburgh. One of the team members who came with them, said, "You're not getting the hint. We really want *you* to be the one to open this office." I was shocked.

Ultimately, after praying about this opportunity, I did apply, interviewed, and was offered the job in 1999. There were many individuals who wanted this job. The reason I know this is because I was given the list of those who applied to be the regional director in consideration of them becoming my deputy director. I was able to assist a large number of individuals in becoming homeowners. My housing plan budget was $2 billion dollars, but we ultimately came under pressure from the Clinton administration to expand mortgage loans to low- and moderate-income borrowers by increasing the number of mortgages in distressed communities as part of the Community Reinvestment Act (CRA) of 1977, which I was charged to do in Southwestern Pennsylvania with national lending institutions. The largest single mortgage transaction I completed with a national multi-billion-dollar bank was $1.11 billion, and my second largest deal was $258 million. This was an unbelievable job, with great benefits, and a mission-minded corporation that allowed me to make a significant difference for many individuals.

When you trust God, He will open doors for you than no man can close. He gave me this job. God is all knowing and all powerful and He is the one who can open the windows of heaven and pour out a blessing you won't have room enough to receive. After seven years, changes in the Congress and Senate meant office closings for Fannie Mae regional offices around the country. But God again opened the doors, and I was offered another job as president and CEO, which I began a few weeks after leaving Fannie Mae, something only He can do. The organization's mission was important to me because we helped individuals who wanted to become first-time homeowners achieve their dream of homeownership.

This is an example of what God does when we give of our time, talent, and resources. He then blesses us with His favor! God was my coach and mentor. I had given what I could, time, money, and service to others, and God opened a door for me of epic proportions.

Chapter 14
Millennials and Generation Z

As stated at the end of the last chapter, I want to share with you some of my research findings from my qualitative dissertation. This data is important, not only for your own benefit and financial awareness, but for future generations, like millennials and generation Z. Even if you don't have children, you probably have nieces and nephews, or maybe know some youth at your church or in your own neighborhood who could benefit from financial education.

As you would expect, the high school students in the summer financial literacy program I initiated at RMU indicated their introduction to finances initially came from discussions with their parents, although other family members were often involved. My co-researchers reported these discussions often occurred in impromptu situations. For many co-researchers, an aunt was a trusted adviser.

While the research indicated these high school students were receiving some financial information regarding money management, it was apparent that the information was not always accurate. The research indicated that some parents had or were experiencing financial challenges themselves. Financial discussions should always focus on a multi-pronged approach and not focus on a single area, such as the financial feasibility of going on a trip. Such an approach does not emphasize the full effect on the importance of savings, budgeting, and the elimination of debt.

The instruction provided by parents is usually well-intended and often has accurate components. It is often devoid, however, of pragmatic reasons of why understanding finances is important. Unfortunately, the majority of high schools have no requirement for students to complete a basic financial education course. They are required to take math but none of these courses teach them basic things like how to balance a checkbook, budgeting, understanding the parameters of credit card debt, student loans, and living on less than you make, which is easier said than done.

Here are nine conclusions I reached based on my dissertation research (I refer to the students as co-researchers).

1. High school students believe understanding finances is extremely important.

This belief was consistent throughout the interviews, although reasons for this belief varied. Success was equated with knowing how to handle money. Several co-researchers believed this so strongly they stated that without knowing how to manage money, they would be "bums on the street," a direct quote from several interviews.

This is the first step on the road to financial literacy, although just knowing it is important, but not enough to become financially astute. What is evident from the research was co-researchers believe that the lack of understanding finances means they will not be successful in life. Therefore, they know it's important to grasp the key concepts of finances.

2. One of the most common financial terms universally understood among the co-researchers was savings.

Savings should be emphasized in the context of short and long-term goals. As impressionable new entrants enter the world of finances, high school students need a comprehensive approach to understand savings. It was clear that if there was any knowledge about finances, it had to do with savings, or savings was at least a part of the discussion regarding finances.

The majority of students believed they were aware of the practice of saving and felt it was important to do. Savings was the most common discussion between parents and their children. It is the easiest concept about finances to understand and requires less money to begin. Saving for the co-researchers occurred in many ways. Some co-researchers used a savings account to save their money. Others had less formal ways to save, such as putting money in places at home where it was easily accessible when needed.

Even though there were constant efforts to save, saving was not about earning interest on the money, but rather it was just a way to put money away. Although earning interest should be discussed, it was almost never mentioned by the co-researchers, an indication of their lack of knowledge about earning interest as a by-product of saving.

3. While no formal training in understanding finances was evident throughout the research, most of the co-researchers knew the ramifications of poor financial choices.

A few students experienced this by watching and listening to their parents discuss past situations, or heard discussions when their parents were attempting to pay their own bills. The discussion of consequences regarding bad debt also left an indelible impression on the students in the context of future opportunities or what having bad debt could do to an individual later in life. None of the students wanted to experience the consequences of bad credit.

This is the reason it is necessary to provide financial literacy education; the co-researchers don't want to be in a bad credit predicament. Without the necessary skills to know how to avoid financial problems, these students were destined to end up where they did not want to be. Minorities have even greater challenges because minority families often have less net worth than do whites. Furthermore, minorities in many cases earn less than whites, Asians, and some Hispanics are sometimes targeted and victimized disproportionately by predatory lenders.

4. Participants did not know what to expect in the training and attended for various reasons, but expected to learn as a result of attending the week-long classes.

Several of the participants had no idea of what to expect in the training, but were excited about the opportunity to participate. While the incentives to learn about finances was important, one participant said their interest in coming was tied to receiving the $325.00 for participating and to open a savings account. Most of the participants truly believed they would gain a greater understanding of finances as a result of participating.

5. The students' exposure to the use of the computer as a technology tool to gain a greater understanding of finances was extremely useful.

A general feeling among the students suggested they believed computers can help and should be used in their quest for increasing their financial knowledge. The use of the computer occurred less frequently for some of the co-researchers because not every family had a computer to use at home. Some of the co-researchers were able to use their school's computers for seeking information.

6. From the research, it has been verified that the majority of high schools do not require any type of money management classes in order for high school students to graduate.

The research provided evidence that the students overwhelming believed that high schools should have some requirement for teaching money management classes. Educators, parents, and those focused on financial education cannot start too early imparting wisdom to high school students.

7. Students had experience using money, and either received an allowance, had a job (mostly part-time) or periodically received money at certain times from their parents (not an allowance) or adult family member.

Irrespective of the income levels of the parents of the co-researchers, there was always some discretionary money that found its way to the students to use as they desired. In nearly all cases, these students had money or access to money to do what they wanted, albeit, it was not a lot of money. Without budgets or financial plans, which was not customary in many of the families' daily financial routine, students used their money for things like shopping at the mall and buying food. In some cases, money was put away in order to have it to spend later on shopping at the mall and buying food.

8. Parents had a strong impact on their children when discussing finances.

Even when parents had financial challenges, their message of "Don't do what I did" resonated with their children. This compelling instruction was the most effective way to get the students focused on the important role of finances in their lives.

A heightened level of awareness regarding the demonstrable lack of financial awareness has become an epidemic. This concern has spawned additional research resulting in the willingness of some educators, retailers, and politicians alike to seek ways to increase the dearth of training in financial management. In the future, if the problem is not dealt with, the implications of this epidemic will impact not only those who may be financially illiterate, but it will have both an immediate and a residual impact on families and society at large, no matter what the income level is.

The economy does suffer because of bad credit choices, which could cost billions over time. Retailers may become more inflexible with credit, a constant fluctuation in interest rates is likely, consumer loans could become more inelastic, and a large part of the consumer market will most certainly have less disposable income to spend.

This research suggests that preparation should occur in multiple forms; there is no one best way to become financially educated. It is also left up to the individual to seek the appropriate tools to become money smart and not to assume they can just figure it out. The groups that may be impacted the most are high school students, which is why a nationwide discussion needs to occur that focuses on the importance of educating the next generation *now*.

This research also clearly demonstrates that a focused strategy of web-based training in as little as one week's time has proven African-American high school students can and will increase this financial knowledge. This research also concluded that the cost and materials needed to provide this training represented a small percentage of most school districts budgets when contrasting it to what can be learned versus traditional education that is devoid of financial literacy training.

If society wants to ensure that the precipitous increase in financial illiteracy slows, it has its greatest chance by requiring high schools to teach financial literacy training. While some adults fall into the category of financially illiterate, the greatest impact will come from working with those who are young and have not yet fallen prey to the predatory heavies of our society. Without formalized methods of training, which includes funding for training and follow-up, the financial illiteracy epidemic, which is now an American epidemic, could grow to be America's greatest epidemic.

It is obvious that our youth need more financial training and their parents often do as well. I have authored this book to contribute toward this need and to foster your ongoing study and education on this important matter. Now, what are you going to do to help?

"You can't be who you're going to be
and who you used to be at the same time."
- Bishop T.D. Jakes

Thematic Perspectives

Thanks for reading my first book. I wrote it to enlighten you and to let you know you can live debt free. It's achievable, no matter what your economic status was or is. I recognize everyone does not aspire to live debt-free and that's understandable, since it's not for everyone. If you have achieved this already, I congratulate you. If you are still on the debt-free trajectory, that's all right too, and if you have been encouraged by my book to start the debt-free journey, that is wonderful news.

I know there are more individuals who are not debt-free than who are. Becoming debt-free produces an amazing feeling, although the next challenge after you are debt-free is to remain debt-free. I can't tell you how many opportunities become available for the debt-free to become in-debt-able again. When you are debt-free and can pay for items you want without borrowing, you'll get more credit-card offers and the interest rate drops precipitously if you want to borrow again (which is a bad idea). Be fore-warned that there will be more distractions along the way. Don't acquiesce to these disruptions.

There have been no absolute rules in this book. I have offered per-spectives, examples, shared ideas, and experiences that I hope have encour-aged you to consider new ways to live in familiar surroundings. Individuals who are debt-free are hard to point out and it's difficult to tell who they are from outward appearances. They often are not flashy, but rather are demure and frugal. They help others, and it's easy for them to live below their means since they have already experienced the debt-free life.

There are numerous ways to achieve this goal and I am not purport-ing to know what they all are. Let me reiterate that this book is not a how-to book, but rather a why-not book. There are few things that everyone must become familiar with in life. Everyone is not required to go to college, everyone is not a professional athlete, and most will never be the President of the United States. Each of us, however, will have to handle money. It's inevitable, and the truth is that some will be better at it than others.

There is no quid-pro-quo to becoming debt-free. It requires work and takes time, strategy, and perseverance, along with a healthy dose of pa-tience. If you have that (the patience, that is), you are almost there. We all have to deal with the vicissitudes of life, but the way to successfully do this is to have faith in God: "Now faith is the substance of things hoped for, the evidence of things not seen" (Hebrews 11:1). A must to get started on the right track is to couple your debt walk with your faith walk; this is the only way to get there.

Remember also, "but without faith it is impossible to please Him: for he that cometh to God must believe that He is a rewarder of them that diligently seek Him" (Hebrews 11:6). The key is to seek God for your way out of debt. Debt has so many negative consequences that it only makes sense not to live in or with it. The prevailing myth, however, is that you can't get out of debt; it's a way of life. While I have a high credit score, these scores are all based on debt and the repayment of that debt. Once my wife and I paid off our debt, we already had a good credit score, but we refuse to go back into debt to increase our scores. Any system that rewards you for borrowing money is not one in which I subscribe to. Moreover, if you have no debt, you don't need a credit score so you can borrow money, and therefore, it's better no matter how you look at it to be debt-free.

Once you achieve debt-free status, it's difficult to go back into debt once you've experienced the freedom that you owe no one anything. Don't be a servant to debt, which is what you are as long as you owe someone else. We all know that people who borrow money are often put in precarious situations as to how and when they will repay the debt. If it's a creditor, you get monthly statements asking for payment and telling you when to pay (I got tired of that). In some cases, the request comes with an attitude: "You must pay by the 12th or we will repossess your car, close your account, or charge you an overdraft fee (too many demands for borrowing $1,000), or will foreclose on your home."

Why in the world would you pay to rent your refrigerator, couch, or television, paying a weekly amount, but never owning? If these companies weren't making money from you, they would not be in the business they are in. You should not borrow from companies, but also refrain from borrowing from an individual. We know sometimes they think they own you when they loan you money; they sometimes call more frequently than traditional creditors to whom you owe a lot more. (By the way, don't ever borrow from family. I get the love between siblings, cousins, aunts, and uncles, but it's too easy to end up on Judge Judy or experience broken relationships. Don't do it!)

As I conclude, it's important for you to know that we are part of a society that embraces debt. We are bombarded daily with ads to encourage us to go into debt. We receive mailers urging us to sign here for debt and we are even told there is good debt. What we don't hear are the problems that families have who struggle with debt, the constant barrage of calls about paying debt, the marriages that fail due to debt, and the lost homes because of too much debt. No commercials I have ever seen express the reality of a person unable to manage their debt. Bankruptcy is marketed as a tool to get out of debt, but speak with someone who has tried to reestablish themselves after going bankrupt, and they will tell you it's not that easy.

My best advice is that you run from debt, not to it, and to know that you can live while debt tries to smother you. It will not happen with the blink of an eye, like *I Dream of Jeannie* or through magic, but rather through your efforts to rid yourself of the debt. If you are not in debt, stay away. If you never become wealthy, you can still live debt free, and that truly is the new American Dream!

"Financial freedom is available to those who learn about it and work for it. Academic qualifications are important and so is financial education. They're both important and schools are forgetting one of them."
- Robert Kiyosaki

BIBLIOGRAPHY

Amadeo, K, (2018), www.thebalance.com Racial Wealth Gap in the United States

Aziz, J. (2014), www.theweek.com How did Americans manage to lose $119 Billion gambling last year?

Badger, E. (2017), www.nytimes.com Whites have huge wealth edge over blacks (but don't know it)

Barry, D. T., Stefanovics, E. A., Desai, R. A., & Potenza, M. N. (2011), www.ncrg.org Differences in the Associations between Gambling Problem Severity and Psychiatric Disorders among Black and White Adults: Findings from the National Epidemiologic Survey on Alcohol and Related Conditions. The American Journal on Addictions

Bennett, M. (2015), www.responsiblelending.org/issues/8-signs 8 signs of predatory mortgage lending

Grant, K. (2017), www.cnbc.com, More Americans are debt free for now

Kantrowitz, M. (2016) www.money.com Why the student loan crisis is even worse than people think

Kiviat, B. (2009), www.content.time.com/time/business The Real Problem with Credit Cards: The Cardholders

Livingston, A. www.Moneycrashers.com How does advertising affect your purchases? – 6 tricks to watch for

Martin, E. (2018), www.cnbc.com Only 39% of Americans have enough savings to cover a $1,000 emergency

Mecia, T. (2018), www.creditcards.com Poll: 2 in 3 U.S. adults with debt doubt they'll ever live debt free

Nolan, H. (2013), www.gawker.com You will not win at gambling

Reynolds, B. (2012), www.washingtonpost.com Minorities fall victim to predatory lenders

Setyon, J. (2016), www.cnsnnews.com// Gallup: Nearly two-thirds of Americans admit they gamble

Smith, L. (2018), www.smartasset.com What is the average savings account balance?

Tepper, T. (2018), www.bankrate.com Most Americans don't have enough savings to cover a $1k emergency

Velez, E.D. (2018), www.forbes.com The U.S. student loan debt crisis is worse than we thought

ConsumerReports.org (2016), www.consumerreports.org/studentdebt

CollegeAtlas.org www.collegeatlas.org (2014), U.S. College Dropout Rate and Other Statistics www.magnifymoney.com (2018), How much does the average American have in savings

The Census Bureau www.nytimes.com (2017), business economy income rebound recession median household income was $59,039

NERD WALLET www.nerdwallet.com (2017), 26 legit ways to make money

www.gobankingrates.com (2016), banking saving-accounts 62-percent american's under 1000 savings

www.insidearm.com/news-experian-announces-sharp-drop (2006), Experian announces sharp drop

www.parade.com Weiss, G., Parade (2008), Don't Get Clobbered By Credit Cards!

www.CNBC.com updated (2010), Defaults bigger threat for the U.S. Economy than terrorism

www.debt.org (2018), Types of debt in America

www.creditcards.com (2018), American's revolving debt, the bulk of which is credit card balances

www.researchgate.net/publication (2014), The influence of advertising on compulsive buying – The role of persuasion knowledge Mikołajczak-Degrauwe, Kalina & Brengman, Malaika ,Journal of behavioral addictions. 3. 65-73. 10.1556/JBA.2.2013.018.

www.creditcards.com (2015), ABA study: Card delinquency stays low

www.consumerReports.org (2016), Degrees of debt and regret

www.Wallethub.com (2019), What is the average credit card interest rate?

www.math.stackexchange.com (2015), Gambling to pay off debt?

www.census.gov/library/publications (2017), Income and Poverty in the United States

www.mydailyinformer.com (2019), 2019-will-be-economically-devastating-for-millions-of-americans

www.scotsmanguide.com/News (2017), African-American-homeownership-falls-to-50-year-low

www.consumerreports.org (2006), Life expectancy of a new vehicle

www.coursehero.com We know there are many cards in circulation

www.forbes.com (2018), Do people really spend more with credit cards

www.globalresearch.ca   Plunder-investigating-our-economic-calamity-and-the-subprime-scandal

www.insidearm.com (2007), Experian's national score index shows

www.debtsteps.com minimum payment credit card calculator

www.forbes.com (2015), racial wealth gap why a typical white household has 16 times the wealth of blacks www.courant.com (2016), ls Consumer Reports College costs

www.washingtonpost.com (2012), minorities fall victim to predatory lenders

www.bankrate.com (2018), banking savings financial security

www.gamblingsites.com (2016), statistics about gambling you need to become familiar with

www.washingtonpost.com (2012), Looking at the status of Black Women

"Before you can become a millionaire,
you must learn to think like one.
You must learn how to motivate yourself
to counter fear with courage.
Making critical decisions about your career, business,
investments and other resources
conjures up fear, fear that is part of the process
of becoming a financial success."
- Thomas J. Stanley

The Biography for
Dr. Howard B. Slaughter, Jr., MBA, MPM

Howard is President & Chief Executive Officer of Habitat for Humanity of Greater Pittsburgh. Prior to joining Habitat, he was an entrepreneur and President & CEO of his own company, Christian Management Enterprises, LLC, a business management and real estate consulting firm. His banking career began at Equibank, where he was an Assistant Vice President. He then became Vice President and Community Reinvestment Act officer at Dollar Bank, where he led the financial institution to its first ever Outstanding CRA rating from the Office of Thrift Supervision.

He was also the Regional Director of Fannie Mae's Pittsburgh Business Center, managing a $2 billion dollar housing investment plan and his office assisted Twenty-Four thousand individuals and families in becoming homeowners during his tenure in Southwestern Pennsylvania. Howard was the first President & CEO of Landmarks Community Capital Corporation, loaning development funding to Community Based Organizations, who were revitalizing neighborhoods. He was also the Chairman of the Urban League of Greater Pittsburgh's Bank on Greater Pittsburgh initiative. He was an Adjunct Associate Professor in the Ph.D. Doctoral (Community Engagement) program teaching Program Development, Evaluation and Assessment and he taught in the School of Business teaching Strategic Management, Introduction to Business and Essentials of Organizational Leadership at Point Park University. He was also an Adjunct Professor at the University of Pittsburgh, where he taught Diversity issues in Public Service and prior to that he taught at Community College of Allegheny County.

In 2017, Howard received a National appointment to the Consumer Advisory Board of the Consumer Financial Protection Bureau, a Governmental Agency responsible for Consumer Protection in the Financial Sector headquartered in Washington, DC. He serves on the boards of the Housing Alliance of Pennsylvania, the Mount Ararat Community Activity Center, the Howard Hanna Free Care Fund Foundation, and the Pennsylvania Economic Development Financing Authority, where he received a gubernatorial appointment to the board from former Pennsylvania Governor Tom Corbett and he's a member of the Operational Committee of the Pennsylvania Community Development Bank. Howard is a former board member and was Chairman of the Policy Committee of The

Pennsylvania Housing Finance Agency, which also included a gubernatorial appointment from former Pennsylvania Governor Ed Rendell, and he's a former Board member of The Pittsburgh Foundation.

He holds an Associate in Science degree in Financial Services, with emphasis on Finance, Insurance & Real Estate from Community College of Allegheny County, a Bachelor of Arts from Carlow University, an MBA from Point Park University, a Master's degree in Public Management from Carnegie Mellon University's H. John Heinz, III School of Public Management and a Doctor of Science degree in Information Systems and Communications from Robert Morris University (RMU). His doctoral dissertation was titled Financial Illiteracy, an American epidemic: A qualitative study on the effectiveness of Web-Based financial literacy technology training on African-American High School students in Pittsburgh, Pennsylvania Copyright © 2006.

Howard received the Outstanding Community Service Award in 2019 from Park Place African Methodist Episcopal Church. He is the recipient of the Carlow University 2017 Laureate Award for outstanding academic achievements and professional contributions of alumni. In 2016, Howard was named one of Community College of Allegheny County's 50 most distinguished alumni. In 2009, he was named a Distinguished Alumnus in the School of Communications and Information Systems at RMU. He also successfully completed the Governing for non-profit excellence program at Harvard University's Graduate School of Business and he completed the Program for Senior Executives in State and Local Government at the John F. Kennedy School of Government, Harvard University. He participated in the Yale CEO Leadership Summit Institute, held at the New York Stock Exchange and completed the Fundamentals of Real Estate Finance course at the Massachusetts Institute of Technology's Center for Real Estate. He is a graduate of Leadership Pittsburgh class 1X and served on its board after completing the program.

Howard is also a graduate of the Defense Equal Opportunity Management Institute, a United States Department of Defense joint service school offering world-class Human Relations education, training and research. He was the keynote speaker at the United States Department of Commerce's Economic Development Administration's East Coast Conference, on the dais with former Philadelphia Mayor, Michael Nutter and former United States Assistant Secretary for Economic Development, the honorable John Fernandez. He is cited in two published books, Cities back from the edge, New life for Downtown written by Roberta Gratz, a former New York Post award winning journalist and Urban Critic and

Changing Places, Rebuilding Community in the Age of Sprawl, written by Carter Wilkie, former White House speech writer and Richard Moe, former President of the National Trust for Historic Preservation.

Howard is a Veteran with two honorable discharges and while in the Navy he was selected to work in the Department of Defense, in the Defense Intelligence Agency at the Pentagon, Washington, DC which required a Top Secret security clearance. He also served in the 479th Field Artillery Brigade in the U.S. Army Reserves. Howard developed and chaired the Minority Research Policy Group of Southwestern Pennsylvania and the all minority Doctoral level participants' initial White paper was titled, Repairing the breach: Setting an Agenda for Social Sustainability Within our Region. Howard was also inducted into his High School Sports Hall of Fame for Football and he is an ordained Deacon and Church Trustee.

"My mom taught me from a young age
to give back and volunteer any chance you get.
It was something that I knew if I made the NFL,
I would financially have the ability to do."
- J.J. Watt

AUTHOR CONTACT INFO

To contact Dr. Slaughter for speaking engagements or seminars, please email him at:

DRHBSJR@gmail.com

or through his publisher at www.urbanpress.us

please visit www.amazon.com to purchase the ebook version of *Addicted to Debt* or for more print copies of this book

Printed in Great Britain
by Amazon